What people are saying about the author

I have read two of Jason Mohaghegh's books prior to reading this work and I find the latter very much in keeping with the author's remarkable voice and almost sui generis approach to and retrieval of contemporary non-western thought. He rather challenges the prevailing contours of philosophy, creatively and philosophically rethinking not only what matters to philosophy but also how philosophy can matter.
Jason Wirth, Professor of Philosophy, Seattle University

Night emerges as an intellectually unique and methodologically courageous work...The author's stylistic and methodological novelty is a great advantage, for it gives the reader, at one stroke, the chaotic and multidimensional universe of culture, and increasingly the world in which we live. It gives us not a clear and transparent unity, a structure, but an ever-changing, fractal cosmos, and invites the reader to follow the trace of the affect in the everyday.
Mahmut Mutman, Professor of Cultural Studies, University of Tampere

T0163420

Night

A Philosophy of the After-Dark

Night

A Philosophy of the After-Dark

Jason Bahbak Mohaghegh

Winchester, UK
Washington, USA

JOHN HUNT PUBLISHING

First published by Zero Books, 2019
Zero Books is an imprint of John Hunt Publishing Ltd., No. 3 East St., Alresford,
Hampshire SO24 9EE, UK
office@jhpbooks.com
www.johnhuntpublishing.com
www.zero-books.net

For distributor details and how to order please visit the 'Ordering' section on our website.

Text copyright: Jason Bahbak Mohaghegh 2018

ISBN: 978 1 78904 277 1
978 1 78904 278 8 (ebook)
Library of Congress Control Number: 2018961966

A CIP catalogue record for this book is available from the British Library.

Design: Stuart Davies

UK: Printed and bound by CPI Group (UK) Ltd, Croydon, CR0 4YY
US: Printed and bound by Thomson-Shore, 7300 West Joy Road, Dexter, MI 48130

We operate a distinctive and ethical publishing philosophy in
all areas of our business, from our global network of authors to
production and worldwide distribution.

Contents

For my wife, the anesthetist, the chef, master of substances, beside whom all nights attain their perfect oblivion.

Introduction

Seven Principles (dark paradoxes)

To study Night, one must stare into what one already realizes intuitively as a paradoxical object: that Night is where horror thrives, and also infatuation; that Night hides certain acts, but that things are also said to "come out at night"; that we are surprised and caught off-guard by its sudden noises, while also recognizing its calm familiarity; and that even Night's mythological child Sleep is no safe bet, dualistically bringing both dreams and nightmares, meaning and nonsense, to the oblivious mind. Beyond this, we must engage Night through the varying prisms of its most fascinating practitioners: namely, those who keep strange hours and navigate the different potentialities of nocturnal experience (both of terror and enchantment). For the criminal's relation to the dark (fugitive, dealer, prowler) is not the same as the wanderer's relation (nomad, sojourner, sleepwalker), nor the many other sub-identities whose survival relies upon a certain exact mastery of Night's formulas and upon learning its conceptual-experiential relations to time, space, fear, nothingness, desire, death, forgetting, enigma, solitude, sensation, vision, secrecy, monstrosity, and the body. To stay vigilant and wakeful throughout; to keep watch while others close their eyes.

Night as Universal Overthrow

Night brings revolution against the archetypal. It overthrows the dominant hierarchies and universal myths in favor of the beautiful disarray of the masquerade or bonfire. It is where one fathoms otherwise, the time-space of the visionary, the imaginary, the unreal, the unknown, the elsewhere, the outside, and the emergent. It is where one first builds machinations of

1

radical thought, letting fall those droplets of mad and dangerous consciousness. The governing categories of human existence are suspended for the meanwhile, and in their place pour forward the semblances of alternative classifications and diagrams (banned libraries, archives, catalogs, arrangements).

There has been an ancient war across the fields of philosophical inquiry, and in this violent conflict two diametrically-opposed sides: on the one front, those movements aligned with perceiving philosophy as enlightenment, and thus inescapably tied to discourses of truth, absolutism, and idealism that would render ours a radiantly serious, legitimate discipline. Tradition, structure, reason, and systemic orders of the mind follow in their wake; and on the other front, those movements aligned with perceiving philosophy as dark trek, and thus inescapably tied to discourses of chaos, exception, obscurity, and fragmentation that would render ours a deviant, criminal enterprise. Originality, distortion, tremor, and rogue speculation follow in their wake. For one alliance, the light promises a certain stability of Being (desire for groundedness); for the other alliance, the night provides gateways and trajectories of becoming (desire for flight or freefall). In this way, it is a war between the throne and the open sea, a war between significance and the ingenious manipulation of meaning within the folds of pure meaninglessness. The conceptual schism between day and night therefore marks the existential border between those with a pathological need to rule and those with a diabolical impulse to abandon, subvert, and reinvent the game of mortal experience.

Night as Fatal Wager

Night is that unique lottery where anyone can win a crucial round, fulfilling otherwise impossible transactions of fortune/ plot if only capable of the right subterfuge. It is where unforeseen cunning triumphs over sober intelligence, where the will to play is rewarded with momentary lawlessness. It is where the guilty are gifted another innocence, and the gods turn blind eyes to those disturbing their cosmos with the gambler's dice. Night thus uproots the origin and installs luck as the new progenitor; it equalizes the board/arena for all malevolent contenders, parting skies for a short epoch of temptation, wonderment, and ecstatic violation of our finitude's limits. It is not the upper air of the sacred promise, but rather the breath of profane eternality lasting only a few stolen hours. It is the site of erased debts and ultimate risk for those with both nothing to lose (desperation) and everything to gain (quest). For this reason, the night is precisely where we perish interminably and yet can never die.

Night as Creational Error

Night is also the time of weeping or celebration for the grand mistake of existence. Creation as error; Being as error. That this should never have happened; that this happened all wrong. That we transpired against odds and intention, in spite of essential forces; that we constitute both symbolic and material offense with every continued breath. Hence night furnishes the precipice across which humanity can take its own insulting presence over and beyond, testing the journey unto a miscalculation's endpoint; it collects tribute for the inexcusability of our arrival herein. Some choose laughter as their vehicle, some choose lament, but all move toward the outer threshold of seeing this fault through…once and for all (the vengeful unwanted). Night thus restores awareness of the longevity of our bondage, and the bondage of our longevity.

Night as Supreme Encounter

Night is where the self encounters its own superior version, whether down some stray alley or in the corner of an old tavern. This figure is the enhanced rendition of one's identity — almost identical but slightly quicker, more eloquent, more attractive, more perceptive. And what does it mean to meet the

3

resemblance that nevertheless always stands two steps ahead? The conditioned subject of the daylight (the social, political, cultural being) would likely fall into immediate resentment and death-wish toward this elevated paragon (don't men kill all their gods, after all?), whereas the nocturnal subject is able to perceive this refined kin as precious to the extent of initiating a relation of immediate discipleship. To kneel before the sharpened counterpart; to bow before one's own arc toward sophistication. Such is the experience of the self's exclusive master whom in midnight hours must be adored, emulated, served, and studied under with consumptive energy. Thus night transforms the typical relationality toward supremacy into one of rightful acknowledgment, restoring one to that most primary honor-principle of wanting to be annihilated by the intensified element of oneself.

Night as Objective Solipsism

Night knows only itself: the dark that admits nothing else, like a black hole permitting no invading light or mass, phenomenologically bound in its own procession. And what happens when a world forgets to host its creatures, forgets everything not properly its own? Beyond immanence and transcendence, we find a solipsistic cruelty whereby the nocturnal no longer recognizes itself in anything else nor anything else within itself. Not even a relation of power, but of indifferent contraction. And yet we would fall lethally if ever placed in the path of such seceding vales, without even the Night's noticing our casualty. We would find ourselves hopelessly evacuated by its interiority, were the atmospheres (the elemental, the terrestrial, the galactic) to claim this right to absolute irresponsibility and self-containment.

Night as First Return

Night in its rarest form is simultaneously an experience of awe (the first time) and return (the revisited). The first return is not primordial but timeless (these are often confused moods, since both feel archaic), a cyclonic sensation—of the circle, ring, whirlpool, vortex, quicksand, and revolving door—for which an inventory of recurrent beings, forces, and attendant concepts proves invaluable:

- Return of the Full Moon (metamorphosis): The Werewolf
- Return of the Nightmare (fright): The Dreamer
- Return of the Sacred (resurrection): The Redeemer
- Return of the Curse (vengeance): The Enemy
- Return of the Tides (migration): The Sailor
- Return of the Banished (hatred): The Exile
- Return of the Ancient (power): The Idol
- Return of the Text (evocation): The Messenger
- Return of the Threat (intimidation): The Extortionist
- Return of the Dead (disappearance): The Ghost
- Return of Desire (obsession): The Stalker
- Return of Pain (infection): The Virus
- Return of the Discarded (waste): The Vagrant
- Return of Glory (vindication): The Fighter
- Return of the Scene (concealment): The Criminal
- Return of Dust (mortality): The Creation
- Return of Instinct (animality): The Creature
- Point of No Return (irreversibility): The Lost Cause

Night harbors all these myriad prototypes in its own creases, allowing us to begin fathoming the further relations of the return to themes of forgetting, innocence, euphoria, disaster, deportation, festival, ritual, cowardice, and obliteration. Such are the mazes hereafter.

Night as Deception Theory

Night solves the paralyzing dilemma of modern philosophy for which the grand challenge to truth, knowledge, and metanarrative appears (to some critics) to have bequeathed a vacuous moment of self-defeating disenchantment. Thought here seemingly deconstructs itself in endlessly self-punishing loops, tearing pessimistically at its own foundations, announcing its frail doubts and qualifying its non-totalizing emptiness, marooned between the unforgiving sands of nihilistic suspicion (toward language, identity, meaning) and the false oases of scientific-epistemological certainty to which some desperately wish their return.

Night, however, provides us with a third route beyond the tabulations of masochistic skepticism and sadistic truth: *deception theory*. It was recognized already in obscure currents of ancient, medieval, and modern thought that the tripartite fatality of essence (death of God, death of the Human, death of the Real) is not meant to incur the dead-end of possibility but rather to blow open a limitless epochal-existential era of lying. The ecstatic convolutions of the lie that exists in no dialectical relation with a truth criterion, the first existential forgery that becomes a thousand branching games of ingenuity, deceit, treacherous play, fictive double-crossing, and elaboration. *"All is illusion, thus all is permitted,"* said the Old Man of the Mountain (leader of the medieval Persian assassins), and no coincidence that such radical utterances occurred amid the fresh air of nights spent walking his courtyards and fortress spires. One could say the constellations carved a slant into his tongue, or that the darkness forked his speech into a smoke-and-mirrors philosophy for the ages. And still it instructs accordingly, reminding us to fill the gaping voids of reason with the farcical-fanatical momentum of vision, slander, rumor, story, and poetic diversion (to become Night's master-liar).

Throughout this short book, we will see how Night provides opportunities for both acute and massive transpositions: in chapter 1, temporal-spatial orders morph into other time-spaces;

in chapter 2, once-presumed identities become contrary personae with their own masks and performative mind-games; in chapter 3, material objects switch places, functions, appearances, and proportions (revenge of the thing); lastly, it is in chapter 4 that concepts themselves bleed and traipse into one another, allowing untold thematic lattices to form. Thus no structure of reality is left immaculate by these better nights; there is only the dampening to concern us here.

Chapter 1

Counter-Futurity (dark time-space): Traveler's Night; Architect's Night; Rebel's Night

Philosophies of night should rightly commence from an awareness of the night-travelers, those who master patterns of nocturnal movement and intricately choreograph their infiltrations or escapes around the hours of mass oblivion. Many conceptual figures rise to the imagination, each with their own techniques, ambitions, and sensorial orchestrations of the dark intervals: The Thief's Night; The Runaway's Night; The Harlot's Night; The Drunkard's Night; The Insomniac's Night; The Revolutionary's Night; The Hysteric's Night; The Sorcerer's Night. All must learn to motion while others fall still; all must grow restless while others stay at rest.[1]

This exploration of the phenomenological-experiential domains of the night-traveler will revolve around two distinct works.

Case 1: B018 Night Club in Beirut, Lebanon (architect: Bernard Khoury, 1998). Situated in a bombed-out, devastated district known as "The Quarantaine" (named after old quarantine sites for foreigners arriving from the nearby port), it later formed the grounds for Armenian, Kurdish, and Palestinian refugee camps cleansed during the country's civil war. Today, this night club is placed underground in the ominous shape of a bunker with a large retractable metallic roof that opens and closes each hour past midnight. So it is that several morphologies of the night-traveler intersect here, both past and present: those of the old boat-passengers once placed under enforced isolation; those of the exiles displaced from occupied homelands; those of the marauding sectarian factions who patrolled city streets each night, opportunistically equating darkness with ideology and blood; those of the slaughtered minorities, who traversed into non-being before the death squads; and lastly, those of our era's night-revelers, who summon themselves to this strange place over and again like a doomsday ritual.

Case 2: Film/Photographic Installation titled *In the Future, They Ate From the Finest Porcelain* (artists: Larissa Sansour and Soren Lind, Palestine, 2016). This visual work stages a fictive dialog between a rebel leader and a psychoanalyst interlocutor, the former charged with "narrative terrorism" for planting false relics in the earth to establish invented histories for a coming people. Hence these two figures—the hooded insurgent and the invisible interrogator—maneuver back and forth tactically across questions of myth, memory, legacy, and power. Here all four concepts are reduced to deceptive art-forms, as futuristic images of desolation loom across the screen. So it is that several morphologies of the night-traveler intersect here as well: those of a militant storyteller transmitting forged messages to descending generations (time-travel 1); those of phantom ancestors and phantom offspring who bind together the strands of a liar's tale (time-travel 2); those of the imprisoned radical pacing through remote, shadow-laced rooms while cross-examined by a voice, an inquisitor obsessed with her origins in criminal warfare (time-travel 3).

1. Night-Travel and Time

B018 is a music club, a place of nocturnal survival.[2]

There are many intricate temporalities woven into the steps of B018's night-traveler: from restive inception to exhaustive aftermath, from the pandemoniac moment of encounter to the minute of futile return.

I. To start from the bookends of this nocturnal process, there are the macro-temporal experiences of entering and exiting which allow the club two separate, mysterious powers: (1) to seal the night-traveler within its own sovereign cube of unworldly time; (2) to then mercilessly release its guests back into the time of the real (last call). These are complex practices aligned with emergent dusk and dawn respectively: first we witness the hyper-anticipatory nervous system of the arrivals, waiting in line outside with rigid postures; then we witness the closing-time eviction, embodied in the slackened torsos of the leaving crowd that resemble zombies staggering into gray sunlight. Thus the once-ancient, nocturnal roles of the lamplighter and the lighthouse-keeper have been translated into their postmodern counterparts of the club manager (who turns artificial light switches to formally inaugurate the nighttime) and the doorman (who scans oncoming presences from near and far). Like all stationed guardians, they literally open and close the gates to a certain exclusive timescape.

II. The next temporal stratum to consider happens inside the club itself, that of the inner-middle experience of the "night out" which passes like an impressionistic sky (liquid or vaporous, without demarcation). They close their eyes; they sway, gesticulate, smile; they drink refined liquors; they feign loss of control. But this is neither transcendent time nor transgressive time; like all decadent modalities, there lies a bitter undercurrent beneath the surface of play; this is why they stage their reverie amid the blast debris of the filthiest district in the city, the gesture itself harboring an element of spite. It is not transgressive because of the non-hierarchical awareness that their entire collective existence is but a mark of evil ruination; it is not transcendent because the slum is the true face of the city. What we get instead is an end-of-the-world show; the time-step of a plague dance.

III. This brings us to our final temporal amalgamation, one that alchemically mixes both the ghost's time and the survivor's time. Let's not forget that this supposed display of the hedonistic present is physically built on the remains of refugee camps liquidated during civil war just one generation prior. Our nocturnal architect, however, has gone to great lengths not to conceal the bullet-ridden apparitions of this obscenity but rather to encase it in the very walls and ground that swallow his patrons each night. The club itself is therefore a blunt force instrument of enunciation of this killing affair; its inexorable electronic beats are pure death rattle. The music funnels back only to the catastrophic imagination; the structure indulges the haunted mind to its nth degree, at once appearing to blend survivor's guilt with the survivor's addictive rush of invincibility. And yet the club's time-game goes even further: for while survival is based on a temporal assumption of the closure of violence (requiring a concept of the elapsed event), this sunken enclosure beneath the earth channels all adrenaline into the disclosure of but one simple fact: that no one made it out alive (the war is not yet over). Yes, there is an error that took place here, and it remains the decried site of error-making. Hence the night-travelers do not raise their glasses in denial; they raise their glasses in recognition of the ever-violating decades, toasting the unforgivable.

1.5 Night-Travel and Time

This place was always a barely functioning dystopia...deeper into the apocalypse, an accelerated microcosm. It disappears little by little.[3]

In the Future, They Ate From the Finest Porcelain introduces its

11

own cauldron of temporal trespasses, those that stretch from primeval wastelands to post-apocalyptic futurities in order to ask us this: How does one establish an immemorial bloodline from the vantage of extinction?

I. The first temporality presented is that of a worn-down fighter confronting the near-erasure of her race. She is a boatwoman rowing against impossible currents; the waters of genocidal certainty close in around her, leaving only a rare semblance of what might be called *failed revolutionary time*. Here time reflects an age of mutual disappearance, and with it the enclaves of an extinguishing present that could not be saved. Her people slip gradually into the open mouth of impermanence—persecuted, transient, unrescued—thereby comprising the formless jawline of lost instances.

II. The second temporality uncovered is that of the non-traumatic recounting of a sister's murder, for which our dissenter narrator describes her as pure scapegoat ("No, in her they saw everyone and everything"). Thus the enemy formations perceived this young girl only through her dangerous potentiality, the next molecules of resistance gestating in her miniature frame, and thus leading us into what might be called *paranoiac time*: that is, a timeframe based on frantic narratives of suspicion, guilt, and pre-emptive punishment. There are no trace-remnants of innocence, not even within the child's body/gaze; all must be taken down, turned into dire example. Even the unborn is classified a threat-in-waiting.

III. The final temporality noted is that of *terroristic time*, though here undertaken as a slow wager across long stretches of civilizational transition. She manipulates destiny; she creates chimeric antiquity for those deprived of name and land. Whereas most terroristic endeavors seize upon temporal blasts of suddenness (surprise, ambush, detonation), this narrative-archaeological version of a woman burrowing crude emblems beneath the dirt in order to win future successors their titles, rights, and authenticity plays into the temporal vastness of the foretold (all that is known is that others will come). Thus political consciousness plunges into the den of cutthroat fantasy images, far-removed from absolute truths and closer to visionary delirium, where it belongs, as the contemporaneous becomes increasingly extemporaneous and the historical becomes strategically cosmological. Only the great dissembler, the falsifier, and the pretender can avenge the marred present, willing geologically-layered illusion upon illusion so as to leave behind a telescopic inheritance.

2. Night-Travel and Space

The opening of the roof exposes the club to the world above and reveals the cityscape as an urban backdrop to the patrons below. Its closing translates a voluntary disappearance, a gesture of recess. The building is encircled by concrete and tarmac rings. The automobiles' circular travel around the club and the concentric parking spots frame the building in a carousel formation.[4]

To understand the spatial dynamics of our first night-traveler typology, one must make a careful inventory of the architectonic features of the B018 spectacle: notably, that of the sector, the staircase, the rooftop, the lot, the tomb, and the target.

I. *Sector*. We must first remember that we are standing in The Quarantaine, a neighborhood originally synonymous with segregation, rejection, stigma, and the millennial fear of the outsider-as-disease. Half a century later, it becomes the abyssal ground for a lethal purging of refugees at the hands of extremist circles, betraying once-sacred oaths of sanctuary and asylum in the name of cruel gods. Thus the site remains scarred by its previous operational logic: half-camp, half-ruin. Today, however, the quarantine sector is known for housing two sensorially-unwanted industries: those of the garbage facilities and the slaughterhouses. Thus the area's perimeter is met always with the wafting odor of animal blood and refuse. It is a place of residual funk, where the dirty work of the city's everydayness gets done off the radar. The trash collector, the butcher: these are the true kings of this domain into which our nightclub-travelers wander. (Side-Note: Just adjacent to the site, not far beyond a few half-condemned buildings, is the ever-idealized presence of the ocean; hence the sound of lapping waves, the smell of salt water, and the vistas of the north Mediterranean coastline commingle at close distance. Consequently, one wonders: Is it wrong for boundless space to be teasingly located at the foot of a carceral/shantytown/killing field?)

II. *Staircase.* There is a clear infernal dimension to the staircase that takes one into B018, like all ladders reaching into subterranean depth, as if the existential cost of the banquet, feast, festival, and masquerade were that of stepping into hell itself. More precisely, though, the lowered concrete staircase acts to conjure reminiscence of the old bombardments, when the city sirens and alarms would announce oncoming air strikes. State of siege; fire raining from smoke-invaded skies. In such instances, one runs instinctually downward for shelter—into the barricade, the trench, the capsule, the chamber—and the club diabolically preserves this impulse, carving visitors into a gesture of emergency confinement.

III. *Rooftop.* The architect tells us that his buildings are "devices," and so we ask what creative stealth is served by a massive metallic roof and its hourly hydraulic retractions. What

14

mechanistic cunning is embedded into this immense contraption that at once protects and exposes the night-travelers to the urban squalor around them? This intermittent revelation signaled by the creaking of steel parts is the antithesis of escapism; the convertible ceiling disallows one from surrendering oneself too completely to the antigravity feeling of the dance and its floating sonic palpitations. It abruptly restores one to the awareness of space-as-armament; not an escape, but rather a sinister tribute to the inescapable (a few seconds delayed).

IV. *Lot.* There is a carnivalesque aspect to the makeshift parking lot which sits on top of the actual club space, like a sculpture garden of abandoned machines placed together in odd striations. This is the "carousel formation" of which the architect speaks. And yet the exceptional stillness of their painted aluminum bodies also gives off a funereal quality, something closer to fossilized bones, as if now deprived of their rightful owners in the wake of an epochal dystopia, leaving only a cemetery or museum of technological archaisms. Is the lot therefore the perfect spatiality of obsolescence, a simulacrum for our surrounding chaos (no driver at the wheel)? On the other hand, one can also read a dark aristocratic atmosphere into the above-ground lot, almost like the parked carriages of a secret society at a secured estate in the woods. An esoteric portal, then, for those dabbling in passwords, occultism, or forbidden services.

V. *Tomb.* To what extent is the club's physical submergence several meters below ground an attempt to transfer its patrons into a mass grave (note its corridors are termed "airlock spaces")? To what extent are these night-travelers participating in the sly brutality of an architect's desire to bury them alive? At the front end, we have a DJ's platform raised up to resemble a colorful altar (though merely caricaturing the absent sacrosanct), and above our heads the corroded roof now seemingly functions as an overhanging coffin-lid. Indeed, the architect speaks further of a certain "macabre aura" to his design, meaning perhaps the very black-humor absurdity that accompanies such night-gatherings: namely, the luxury of slightest fortune through which some have persisted semi-breathing amid the many mounds of an otherwise exterminative modernity.[5] And yet this half-life does not sit well with them, the night-travelers; hence they come to B018 to finish the job. A quest for finality itself, once and for all: the compound of a suicide cult.

VI. *Target*. From an aerial perspective, the club's architectural blueprint resembles nothing less than the crosshairs of a sniper's rifle, such that all visitors stray into the fatal universe of the target. The structure therefore finds itself at the epicenter of a bad aesthetic omniscience, its inhabitants unified beneath the bull's-eye and the malevolent will of a draftsman-turned-marksman. And when spat back out eventually into the bleak dawn of 7:00 a.m., they physiologically exemplify this assault (of the hunter's night): the once-fashionable re-emerge looking ill-fashioned, victims of a becoming-unbeautiful...their hair disheveled, their cosmetics streaking, their clothes stained by promises of false excess. They are no longer elite, but rather exude profanation; they stagger gracelessly and perplexed like the first human beings, or someone shot through multiple limbs, or something larval and half-blind. The target has therefore escorted them either toward pure infancy or pure terminality, their exceptionalism/identity forfeited underground. They all look alike now beneath a weak sun, recollecting for us the expression "dead ringers" often mistakenly attributed to the practice of placing a bell-cord in fresh tombs just in case the subjects were mistakenly interred while comatose/sleeping so that they could rouse others to unbury them (thus the properly-ascribed expression, "saved by the bell").[6] But salvation does not make rounds to The Quarantaine, as the final bell-toll of

B018 does nothing but send its consumers reeling into vampiric vulnerability, hyper-sensitive to certain forms of light, touch, and sound, so dead inside as to attain accursed immortality, and thereby paying the fair price of a night's thirst...the disgraceful reminders of creation's mistake.

2.5 Night-Travel and Space

It gets dark early here in the desert. There's no artificial lighting for miles.
But you are no longer in the desert, remember?[7]

To understand the spatial dynamics of our second night-traveler typology, one must make a careful inventory of the architectonic features at work in the filmmaker's piece: notably, that of the continual oscillation between desert (as colonized infinity) and darkness (as hostile reflection).

I. *Desert (horizon)*. The first image of the film is an eerie shot of several interplanetary trailers parked in rows across some frontier outworld, each one gradually hovering then departing the red sands. Their exodus-into-flight returns us to the simplicity of scorched-earth terrain contrasted against a dim-lit sky, leading us to recognize our preliminary spatial checkpoint as that of an occupied horizon (infiltration of clouds, mist, untouched ridges). All subsequent images to follow will be appropriately horizontal, i.e. caught within the compulsive horizontality of conquest and territoriality: the mapmaker's latitudinal web; the imperialist's drive toward universality and world-making.

II. *Darkness (locked room)*. We are then transported elsewhere, into a closed darkroom where our narrator (the rebel leader) makes her way with calm, audible steps toward the watcher's vantage. The space is locked, forming an echo-chamber; the darkness around her creates a tight ethereal border, forcing her to walk in linear, spotlighted strides. She herself is a white-hooded figure, until raising her eyes to meet ours, a hollow-point encounter with faciality/gazing for which she holds the perceptual advantage. She wins the stare-down easily: for she knows why she is there, and we do not; furthermore, she knows exactly what side she is on, her chosen stance and belonging, while we remain clueless to where we stand in this narrative (accomplice, conspirator, traitor, ally, adversary?).

III. *Desert (oasis)*. We shift instantly into a memory/photograph of an oasis with two young girls in traditional Arabic clothing at the center; to their right, two bearded nomadic men sitting cross-legged on the ground; to their left, the gray-tinged specters of three western settlers. As we approach a close-up of the two girls' faces, their gowns (*kaftans*) turn increasingly crimson and then indigo; each inhales deeply and opens their eyes in slight amazement, as if shaken awake from a dream or resurrected. Necromantic touch: they look around themselves uncomfortably, sensing the total defamiliarization of this once-familiar setting, in wondrous realization that their home is no longer theirs. This is complemented by the later image of the hooded rebel (presumably one of the former youths) now standing in the same spot holding a shovel before a giant hole, and surrounded by uniformed colonial officers (weapons across shoulders), the native men and adolescents since eviscerated from the scene. Her little sister's grave, or an excavation site; meant to hide collaterally-damaged bodies or to extract valued resources? Either way, it is now the space of voluminous betrayal.

IV. *Darkness (salt table; deathbed)*. We return to the darkroom that somehow navigates between claustrophobic moodscapes (fear of enclosure) and claustromaniacal moodscapes (love of enclosure). For while the psychoanalyst's interview proves grueling, it also illuminates the broader impasse resting before the game's opponents: no, our militant protagonist is not broken down, challenged, or coerced into confessional surrender; rather, her answers drift forward with an air of trivial explanation of the unfathomable (the other will never understand this). As if to render an accurate phenomenological manifestation of this triviality, we then find a recurring image of what appear as salt piles strewn across the table like scaled-down, miniscule mountains. The hooded insurgent suspends herself awhile above the fragile granular formations, only later to confirm that the table's salt heaps in fact comprise a subtle fabric; she reclines beneath it, draped in the delicate linen cloth of the region's dead, reminding us that only the child/animal plays mimetically at sleep or death. Thus the psychoanalyst rightly observes that, "You were talking about being buried as part of your own fiction," to which she responds, "Right. I often picture myself draped in cloth on my deathbed...becoming my own civilization's Shroud of Turin."[8] Thus the space of the salt table becomes the space of the deathbed.

V. *Desert (the elders; the rains; the towers)*. There are several visions of colossal desert landscapes that hereafter advance in harsh succession, two of which fall under a similar classification: the first is of an aged tribal woman with pipe and headdress staring outward as wisps of smoke blow mournfully around her; the second is of an aged tribal man with white beard, turban, and maroon robe peering into the camera lens while encircled by tents and parachuting bombs. These are the elders, those casualties of forsaken/razed spaces now condemned to images of an ethnographic façade (photographs of communal grimness). Both possess an almost sage-like composure, aware of the disaster to befall their kind ("in times of quiet, we once again cease to exist").

The next image is of our hooded rebel standing in an open field beneath falling shards of porcelain, for which she constructs the following pronouncement: "Sometimes I dream of porcelain falling from the sky, like ceramic rain. At first it's only a few pieces falling slowly like autumn leaves. I'm in it, silently enjoying it. But then the volume increases, and it's a porcelain monsoon, like a biblical plague."[9] There is an initial pleasure to the glass-rain particles, a mild ecstatic potential that then goes too far (into celestial disturbance), becomes an unbearable flood of solidity as space turns sharp, scabrous, fragmentary. She shields herself against the brittle downpour, clasps ears and head while unable to block out the acoustic attack of shattering pieces. Such is the affective mosaic of the Unstoppable (here as spatial paragon).

Lastly in this sequence, we find a captivating image of the earth littered with endless shells, plates, and stones. As the camera motions skyward, we see the fractal path leading toward the silhouettes of a faraway city with jagged towers and spires. Indeed, the new metropolises will ravage all past worlds, prompting us to speculate about its crucial repercussion: Will the former savage (ignorant of civilization) now become the barbarian (nemesis of civilization)? Solitary space hereafter transforms into combative space.

VI. *Darkness (hole).* Cellars of horrific recovery (of what should remain irrecuperable). Here we watch the hooded rebel's recurring nightmare: she is standing above the cavernous hole to find her little sister huddled at the bottom, clutching knees to chest, trembling against the full pressure of the cylinder (density of the nothing). But this is not the true source of horror; it is the vacant mental lapse that brings overwhelming fright, for she remembers nothing. This hole is the very isle of a child's amnesia, where forgetting itself takes on a viscous materiality: "She does not recognize me. She cannot communicate with the future."[10] Space as oblivion spell.

VII. *Desert (circus; anti-feast)*. The final two desert images concerning us are themselves examples of visual finality. The first picture is that of a Ferris wheel making its gentle rotations in the middle of nowhere, a ticket booth stationed randomly at its side; it is the carriage of a universal miscarriage, the ride of cyclical annihilation and annihilative cyclicality. Twilight, barrenness, aridity, and a lone circus amusement: such a likeness of apocalyptic saturnalia (too-late spatiality), a last game and merriment before the end of all things.

The second image is the actual closing picture of the film itself: it depicts a clear imitation of the last supper, our now saint-like rebel flanked by seated missionaries and colonial overlords. But what does this portrait signify here, less a pre-crucifixion rite of commemoration (among disciples) than a symbol of martyrological infection (against enemies)? Does she mean to devour these world-historical raiders (eating alive) or to afflict their species (contaminating throughout)? The chalices and white trays serve mostly emptiness save a few indistinguishable droplets and slices (of blood, flesh?). Either way, the anti-feast delivers its retributive message without mistake: that this reception will take eternal residence in their veins (final dromological phase: intravenous travel), entering bloodstreams without redemptive intent; perhaps instead, her sacrifice will form the corrosive alcohol of livers or acidic bile of spleens. Insurrectionary night; space of toxicity, fifth-column trickery, assassin's motive.[11]

3. Epilogue: Night-Travel and the Last Movement
The dividing-line between "pleasure" and "release from pain" grows murky in the entertainment quarters, and it grows equally murky in the areas of collective revenge. Hard to tell where one ends and the other begins, or whether they indeed form a

regenerative loop that fuses euphoria, spite, and an inhuman will to disappearance. On the one side, there are the night-travelers of intoxication who engage in a club's weekly ceremony of showmanship, expenditure, and energetic squandering. Their movements are those of flailing bodies and pseudo-orgiastic overlap amid rhythms pounding from the center of the earth. On the other side, there are the night-travelers of fatigue and insularity, those who live in dunes of chronic war and therefore discipline themselves in the elaborate practice of riot, sedition, sabotage, and treason. Their movements are those of fatalistic slowness, pensive shuffling or still-life paralysis, and then devious subversion. The drunkard's dance illustrates the nothingness in excess; the rebel's strike illustrates the excess in nothingness. The first hides its poverty in a theater display of the euphonious (flagrant sound) and the diaphanous (flagrant light); the second hides its rich vitality in the silence, long pauses, and constrictions of a torture chamber or burned village. One feigns iconographic writhing; one feigns dreadful immobility. But both are expert performativities of the night-traveler; both require a profound alignment with nocturnality and dark power in order to cross safely; and both produce their own low-laying trances, the time-space when enchantment and disenchantment fall into seamless explosivity.

Concept Map (of the Counter-Futural Night; dark time-space)

TIME 1
Unworldly Time (entrance, exit)
Impressionistic Time (decadence, ruination)
Catastrophic Time (the ghost, the survivor)

TIME 1.5
Revolutionary Time (failure)
Paranoiac Time (scapegoat)
Terroristic Time (chimera)

SPACE 1
(the sector) (the staircase) (the rooftop) (the lot) (the tomb) (the target)

SPACE 1.5
Desert
(the horizon) (the oasis) (the elders) (the rains) (the towers) (the circus) (the anti-feast)

Darkness
(the locked room) (the salt table) (the deathbed) (the hole)

MOVEMENT 1
(euphoria) (intoxication) (expenditure) (dance) (writhing) (ceremony)

MOVEMENT 1.5
(spite) (fatigue) (insularity) (slowness) (paralysis) (subversion)

B018 Night Club. Beirut, Lebanon. (Architect: Bernard Khoury; Built 1998).
© DW5 BERNARD KHOURY—Photos by IEVA SAUDARGAITE

In the Future They Ate From the Finest Porcelain, film, 29 minutes, Larissa Sansour/Soren Lind, 2016.

Chapter 2

Inexistence (dark figures): Elder's Night; Sleeper's Night; Madame's Night

A poetess who had died young of cancer had said in one of her poems that for her, on sleepless nights, "the night offers toads and black dogs and corpses of the drowned."
Yasunari Kawabata, House of the Sleeping Beauties[12]

The Inexistent Night is the anti-archetype of a lost night, forgotten night, or night that never should have happened. No others know what transpired then; they will never learn of the things done in that dark heaven when no one was looking. For the inexistent night stands outside of chronology, identity, and judgment, an unaccounted mood through which certain figures/ creatures actualize their disappearance...whether for a short while or forever.[13]

Narrative Premise: A 67-year-old man walks the late-hour streets of Tokyo to visit a nameless inn where he can lay beside young women placed into deepest sleep states. They are drugged with an unknown medicine and situated in rooms where the old men undress and quietly slip into beds beside them for the night's stretch.

This forms the operational setting of Yasunari Kawabata's obscure short novel titled *House of the Sleeping Beauties*, a minimalist tale of aged personae with no greater wish than to die while resting adjacent to comatose feminine partners. Together, they enter slumbers that should not be admitted; but beyond this simple collaboration awaits a cabinet of curiosities or Pandora's Box of subjects, objects, atmospheres, associates, and body parts. They require a conceptual map to configure their complex implications, a map of the inexistent night.

Let there be no misunderstanding: at first glance, this is a profoundly distasteful text, laced with tinctures of sadism, patriarchal authority, and even the fascist compression of living subjects into soulless automata. But it also troubles this critique by pulling everything into the labyrinth of not a genocidal conclusion but rather ontocidal conclusion (the decimation of Being, both individual and universal). As such, there is a new alterity to be discovered in these altercations with the fast asleep. The deed is not something *nefarious* (meaning "against divine law," related to the Latin or Greek root "I say/speak"), for the characters here remain unspeaking throughout and therefore irrelevant to the demands of any sacred tongue. Rather, the Old Man and his unconscious courtesans are co-conspirators. She is the rejection of him; he is the rejection of her. He finds the distillation of his own reversal in her closed eyes. They are each other's malfunction, and do their negative bidding. Half-revenant; half-detritus.

The Old Man
1. Watcher (distance, fascination)

Her forehead came against his eyes. His eyes were closed, and he closed them tighter.
Behind the closed eyes an endless succession of phantasms floated up and disappeared. Presently they began to take on a certain shape. A number of golden arrows flew near and passed on. At their tips were hyacinths of deep purple. At their tails were orchids of various colors.[14]

Let us begin with the Old Man: fittingly, his first typology is that of the Watcher, possessed by a low-intensity impulse to stare upon the sleeping beauties in their rest states. Thus he is a figure tied to concepts of distance and meek fascination.

From his first steps into the strange house, the Old Man

27

proves tentative; his initial exchange with the inn's Madame is brief and tensely worded; he barely speaks except to respond, confirming his understanding of basic guidelines while averting his eyes from direct confrontation. First paradox of the Watcher: that to master gazing, one first masters avoidance of the world's gaze upon oneself (the Watcher who is never watched).

She leads him into the transitional parlor preceding the bedroom of the first sleeping beauty, whereupon he immediately falls into states of vigilance, noting every small artifact of his surroundings: the decorative bird stitched onto the Madame's traditional robe; the sound of wind and waves outside crashing against nearby cliffs; the particular species of wood forming a partition between himself and the secret bedchamber of the young woman. Maximal optical precision and phenomenological attunement: he feels warmth; he listens to weather; he attends to the careful placement of items. He does not conquer; he studies. Second paradox of the Watcher: that the hyper-subjective impulse to consume the other's form (here visually) begins from an enhanced sensitivity toward the objective universe of things (the Watcher who gains awareness of all but himself).

The Madame then leaves the Old Man alone, handing him the key to the next room where this rare indulgent fantasy plays itself out night after inexistent night. The next moments are crucial in solidifying this voyeuristic phase of consciousness: for he halts himself, and in this single precious hesitation he discovers the correct framework of immersive experience. Let us follow him in his essential paces: he first sits down, lights a cigarette, hardly smokes before smothering it, lights another, smokes it to completion, recites a morbid line of poetry, dwells in faint philosophical contemplation of the room's emptiness, and finally speculates on the potential ugliness of the sleeping beauty on the other side of the screen. Pausing, ritual kindling and extinguishing, inhalation of foreign substances, engagement of philosophical-poetic modes, and the pre-emptive envisioning of the event-to-come at both its most radiant and grotesque fulfillment. Third paradoxes of the Watcher: that the ecstatic height of desire occurs not in consummation but in the anticipatory gradient just beforehand, and that extreme curiosity inspires one to traverse reality and map the entire realm of potentiality from a close distance (the Watcher who imagines all possible rooms before entering the actual room before him).

The Old Man slides beneath the covers and begins staring intently at the physical features of the first sleeping beauty offered to him, though his meticulous cataloging of anatomical details serves only as the obvious task behind which a more insidious power gathers. No, such myriad peculiarities (her outreaching wrist, her unpainted eyebrows and even eyelashes, her youthful jawline) only serve the function of catalyst or contagion for the Watcher's final transformative victory: in effect, the hallucinatory importation of the external object of captivation. Thus her mystifying presence evokes a coterminous mystification of the inner provinces of thought and imagination, to the extent that the Old Man closes his eyes to witness multicolored arrows shooting through black interior/cosmic space. It is the severe twisting of perception itself, the contortion-unto-awe, that we are after here, and with it an adeptly-done trick of simple yet measureless proportions. For the one who can train themselves into all-embracing fascination can thereafter enable almost any passing form to induce elusive, drug-like effects. Fourth paradox of the Watcher: that the transfixed gaze on outer worlds functions as a distorting mirror to ignite disquieting shapes in the inner world, binding what transpires beyond and beneath the looker's eyelids in a dance of absurd marvel (the Watcher who holds keys to immanent altered states).

2. Deviant (violation, play)

He was not yet a guest to be trusted. How would it be, by way of revenge for all the derided and insulted old men who came here, if he were to violate the rule of the house?[15]

The Old Man cannot remain the Watcher forever, and thus gradually metamorphoses into a second typology of the Deviant, conceiving those small delightful trespasses to be entertained in his time beside the sleeping beauties. Thus he is a figure tied to concepts of violation and play.

There are three levels at which the Deviant operates herein, the first of which involves childlike practices. He wonders about silly antics and acts of frivolous discourtesy, like the placing of fingers in facial orifices or the flicking of the other's teeth. These are nothing more than mild organic adventures, slight fallaways from respectable ordered culture, always short-lived and barely subversive movements against codified behavior. But there is also something significant in the switch, as the Old Man sheds legitimate conduct (custom) in favor of trivial gestures (whim), a first recognition of the Deviant: that to disrupt the rules of the game implicitly acknowledges existence as mere game, and all aspects therein as game pieces (deviancy as expert cheating).

The second level of the Deviant concerns erotic practices, and indeed the Old Man's mind insistently returns to the threshold of the inn's supreme rule: to desist from sexual impositions. Such is the forbidden fruit of this particular night-garden, the source of angry tirades and the Old Man's constant will to defiance (though he never crosses its limit). Rather, his compulsive fixation with the rule's vulnerability is sufficient to break certain spells (of the real) while pronouncing certain others (of the inn), its recurring potentiality enough to combine: (1) the existential freedom experienced by the cliff-walker; (2) the narcotic apathy experienced in ancient mythologies of the lotus-eaters. The first figure (of the edge) recognizes that no intervening power structure can prevent one from stepping forward into pure freefall, if one so wishes (the unobstructed); the second figure (of the island) grows increasingly careless toward ever wanting to escape, having no greater wish than to remain (the unmindful). Thus the erotic faculty at once fuses vertiginous animation with paralytic bliss, which is why the Old Man often tosses and turns for hours without ever really leaving the bed. The permissive, the ensnared: a perfect tempo between expulsion and gagging achieved by the inner circle of our text's actors. Eros is now an influence-peddler that unfastens one from the world's oppression precisely by chaining one to the outworld's temptation, the slow-twitching bodies of the sleeping beauties functioning like the wound and unwound springs of a clock on the other side of the earth. The old man is liberated (nothing could drag him away from this place); the old man is helpless (he cannot tear himself away from this place). Second recognition of the Deviant: that ultimate desire forms an adaptive consortium between the spirit of rebellion and complacency (deviancy as insurgent forgetfulness).

The third level of the Deviant mutates toward vampiric practices, entering into an amoral logic of transfusion that brings no less than the end of transgression itself. There is no longer an abstract moral boundary at stake, but rather just a visceral urgency to snatch youth and trade back immortality (amid gnashing fangs). Note the reciprocal double-bind of this commerce enacted by a single shared bite: first he imbibes the other's mortal vitality; then he pours ageless calm into her veins. Yes, the sleeping beauties are themselves also recipients of an unparalleled substitution, gaining seasoned wisdoms, teachings, and sensitivities far beyond their years. This is how they join an elite bloodline. The everlasting, the forthcoming: these are the last bonds conveyed by the aberrant, the divergent, the ones of irregular tastes. Third recognition of the Deviant: that this

31

piercing transfusion of dual life (both finite and eternal) forms a circular current, on one side winning perpetuation for an outlawed, predatory race always on the brink of thirstlessness and, on the other, winning destiny for an elect group of night-mistresses always on the brink of neglect/emergence (deviancy as mutual vivification).

3. Warlord (cruelty, anger)

She would probably not go on sleeping if, for instance, he were to cut her arm almost off or stab her in the chest or abdomen.

"You're depraved," he muttered to himself.

Thoughts of atrocities rose in him: destroy this house, destroy his own life too...[16]

Later we find the Old Man wearing his third mask of the Warlord, designing brutalities and contemplating tactics of smothering, bleeding, and poisoning the sleeping beauties. Thus he is a figure tied to concepts of cruelty and anger.

The exact techniques of this Warlord mentality are blatant enough to compile: strangulation, amputation, incision. This is how a feeble person encourages himself to become the Deliberate One, first by perceiving all action as an overture to the razing, dissection, demolition, or dismantling of forms. In this respect, they are the exemplar of formlessness attained by malevolent means. They restore war to its most fundamental gesture, unadorned by ideological justifications: to break worlds. This is the antithesis of the world-building imperialist: for while empire seeks absolute unification, the Warlord's quest is to create an increasingly fractal map—endlessly branching borders running like constricted spider-veins across the parchment. The flesh of the sleeping beauties is but the chosen theater of battle through which divisional cartographies take hold, forcing us to re-envision them not as pure victims but as pure weapons or arenas (of space-shattering).

Pay no attention to the apparent inaction of the whole body; instead, pay attention to the throbbing micro-lacerations and miniature puncture-wounds behind the ears and under the scalp's hair. This is no pantomime, and the sleeping beauties are not useless shells; rather, the Warlord is on a heathen's mission to find something invaluable: namely, the one who can authentically kill him, and on his best night. His saber-rattlings are therefore meant to rouse and rile the different women to awaken, strike fatally, and thus seal a homicidal pact. Correlational malice; rotating malefactors; familial evil. He craves his own nemesis star; he dares the true enemy to escape sleep's clutches and sink their young white nails into his undoing (bringers of finality).

4. Dying Man (eventuality, surrender)

Ah! The curtains that walled the secret room seemed the color of blood. He closed his eyes tight, but that red would not disappear...His conscience and his reason were numbed, and there seemed to be tears at the corners of his eyes.[17]

So it is that the Old Man becomes the fourth paragon of the Dying Man, recognizing his imminent terminality and wondering whether each night spent in the remote inn might prove his last. Thus he is a figure tied to concepts of eventuality and surrender.

The thoughts of the Dying Man grant an interesting moratorium: the mind intones lowliness; the mind becomes an oblique compromiser; the mind embarks upon a black-hearted study of skin-shedding. In this way, he draws the sleeping beauties into the malady of a collective solipsism (where only two or three at a time participate in an otherwise solitary, self-contained world). They join him in the outworn and the anachronistic; they become equal candidates of good riddance, presenting their bodies as recipient satellites or stations of conjugal draining. To what end, though?

The Dying Man is the agent of a certain sadness, and hones the shifting skyline of disappointment in each nightly encounter. But these slight pangs are neither tragedy nor melancholy, for both prove discourses too immense for this small overlooked inn, this narrow room, this cramped bed. Rather, the old men here salute a minor death, the lame exit of just someone left behind, and the young women are not (despite appearances) sold items but instead master purchasers/barterers who effectively cheat their own one-time death via the all-night dying of their elder bedmates. The old men are lost-in-time eccentrics, and thus introduce the sleeping beauties to a dark-horse temporality (of the million-to-one shot); they make the mortal payment on the fairer ones' behalf, allowing them to skip their turn perpetually (without yesterday or tomorrow). This is the exquisite deal: one surrenders to chronic perishing, and the other attains imperishability (to step beyond *chronos*). All are extortionists here.[18]

The Sleeping Beauties

Let us turn now to the sleeping beauties themselves. While they are often mistaken for mere dolls of absolute passivity, they in fact react sensorially to every touch, voice, and climate. They are not unresponsive, but rather form lean conductive channels of enthusiasm, synergy, and even biomimicry that stretch between their pale limbs and those of the elder visitors. Thus we must dare to advance a theory of unconscious intimacy harbored by these scarcely-living entities, for each sleeping beauty exudes her own potent effects.

To correctly interpret the sleeping beauties requires a sensitivity to the most torpid, idle, languid, stale or stony, insensate, or insentient forms. It requires an ability to read the tiniest flecks and tinges, the unbelievable subtlety of the movement-in-sleep. They are not truly petrified; they are histrionic, like those gargoyles whose radically intimidating potential is encapsulated in their horrid stillness. Yes, the sleeping beauties are figures of semi-frozen majesty who turn their beds into gaming-tables and safe-houses; they perform armed robbery of the fantastical, hiding in plain sight; they use their lactic and sanguinary fluids like potions of illicit substance; they supervise the three stages of twilight (civil, nautical, astronomical); they simultaneously induce phronemophobia (fear of thinking) and phronemomania (rapture of thinking); they make all newcomers envious, and promise no utopia, but rather only scotopia (night vision).

1. Guide (portal, initiation)

Though this girl lost in sleep had not put an end to the hours of her life, had she not lost them, had them sink into bottomless depths?..No, not a toy; for the old men, she could be life itself. Such life was, perhaps, life to be touched with confidence... In taking his hand from her neck, he was as cautious as if he were handling a breakable object.[19]

The first sleeping beauty is a Guide, in that she discreetly draws the Old Man into the folds of peaceful oblivion and acquaints him with the ways of death-like sojourn. Thus she is a figure tied to concepts of the portal and initiation.

The Guide must indoctrinate clients into a theo-perceptual order of henotheism or monolatry (the worship of a single deity, though recognizing the potential existence of other deities). For this is what transpires each night in the inner chamber: the Old Man submits himself before a different exclusive subject of adoration, while keeping in mind the continued presence of other sleeping beauties hovering roundabout. Thus the Guide brings him into a hermetic queendom where loyalties shift and obsessive devotion switches from one face to another at various turns. Moreover, we are given hints of a backdoor temporal deal whereby hours "sink into bottomless depths," forcing us to weigh the implications of thinking time not as progressively linear but rather vertical, and even beyond verticality given the elimination of any foundational ground or footing. Does depth become a phenomenological something-else once infinitized downwardly (descending eternality), leaving no borders but rather only perpetual states of diving, tumbling, plunging?

The Guide must also present her own corporeal frame as emblem for the fragility of all living things ("a breakable object"). Touch enables the Old Man to grasp this notion (violence of the hands), and to recognize how the sheer tremulous frailty of our being overrides any transcendent discourse of control, sovereignty, individualism, or consent. This gentle, affectionate theft of insusceptibility and laying humankind bare upon the agape cradle/mattress of existence; this radical openness/wretchedness that paradoxically bestows "confidence" upon her newest initiate.

2. Witch (magicality, seduction)

Her face, now turned toward him, was too near, a blurry white to his old eyes; but the too-thick eyebrows, the eyelashes casting too dark a shadow, the full eyelids and cheeks, the long neck, all confirmed his first impression, that of a witch.[20]

The second sleeping beauty is the Witch, in that something about her raises suspicions of trickery, evil, and otherworldliness. Thus she is a figure tied to concepts of magicality and seduction.

The Witch's body is a grimoire (book of instructions about magical objects, beings, and practices); her breathing patterns are themselves invocations (of what hidden spirits or spiritlessness?). The first indication of this status rests in the above passage, for it speaks of her as a force of proximate stupefaction: namely, being at once "too near" and yet coated in "blurry white" contours that thwart recognition, discernment, or classification (everything a thaumaturgic spindle). She steals into closest quarters without detection, resurrecting a long-standing thematic through which imperceptibility (of movement, reason, name) has always been associated with evil practice. She is also given the true mark of monstrosity—physiological excess—through which bodily features grow to exaggerated, alarming extremes (the vampire's fangs, the crone's nails, the werewolf's hair). Thus the unmistakable references to the lavish thickening, darkening, filling, and lengthening of proportions or appendages, a vital procedure through which once-normal traits achieve pathological abnormality. Each perverse dimension of appearance in turn echoes some worst-case intentionality, signs of the creature's capacity for extended disfigurement (both inner and outer), and with this a simple lesson linking maleficence to exacerbation: that all one needs is to take things slightly too far, and entire past worlds of definition fall apart.

3. Innocent (doubt, manipulation)

The small girl had a small face. Her hair, disheveled as if a braid had been undone, lay over one cheek, and the palm of her hand lay over the other and down to her mouth; and so probably her face looked even smaller than it was. Childlike, she lay sleeping.[21]

The third sleeping beauty is the Innocent, in that we meet her on her first night at the inn, reading that she enters this new profession with misgivings and cautious thoughts. Thus she is a figure tied to concepts of doubt and manipulation.

The Innocent is the insinuation of a mordant birthright; the sprawling limbs and "disheveled" strands of hair are themselves performative emulations of the first of our race, those primal amateurs of just-emergent consciousness who shuddered and cowered beneath the immensity of sheer being. She reminds us of the grand shame of our species' beginning in pure terror; her fear is the original fear of the ancestor. But the Innocent's return to all-encompassing doubt is also the guarantor of her manipulative talent, for she is somehow able to look "even smaller" than her actuality, to strategically simulate infancy or infinitesimal contraction. She is the radical inverse of the Witch's flagrancy, which attains repulsive perplexity through overproduction; instead, hers is the more subdued gift of the unsuspecting, which wins attractive clarity through diminution. She masters affectations of the harmless ("childlike"), she allows her arms and legs to twirl around in demure disarray, thereby allowing us to underestimate the danger of little-seeming things.

4. Recollector (image, return)

He lay for a time with his eyes closed, for the girl's scent was unusually strong. It is said that the sense of smell is the quickest to call up memories; but was this not too thick and sweet a smell?..From ancient times old men had sought to use the scent given off by girls as an elixir of youth.[22]

The fourth sleeping beauty is the Recollector, in that her own demeanor submerges the Old Man in a flood of past memories. Thus she is a figure tied to concepts of the image and the return.

The Recollector's scent is described as an "elixir": from the Arabic al-iksir and Greek xerion, meaning "powder for drying wounds." Furthermore, it is a favored concept of the alchemists, for whom genius always rests in distortional capacity (techniques of modulation, reversal, effacement). So what is the exact wound and what is the particular metamorphosis of which our fourth sleeping beauty partakes? That she "calls up" various scenes is our first clue, something akin to summoning or even conjuration masquerading as reminiscence. For we are never quite assured that these indeed represent his personal memories; more intriguingly, they may be the impersonal likenesses of others who have washed in and out of the inn, the neighborhood, the city, or even the earth. These images lodge themselves in his mind, taking on a quality of intimate foreignness.

She alone endows such hindsight of unrelated events, for she seems the scavenger of past incidents, managing a mercurial recurrence; she is a cistern holding myriad unclaimed contents, the procession of certain heights and failures; she perhaps makes her bedmate confiscate predicaments that do not belong to him, to host apparitions not his own. The silhouette; the chimera. No, we should not mistake these flooding "memories" as proper traces or hauntings of the Old Man's nostalgia, since their biographical accuracy remains in question, but instead accept the dire possibility of his recollecting things before himself, behind himself, beyond himself, outside himself ("from ancient times"). Segments of alien experience; glimpses of strangers' nights, closer to spasmodic intuition or even partial omniscience (to see portions of others' lives whenever closing one's eyes).

5. Dreamer (vision, restlessness)

She was perhaps frowning, but it also seemed that she was smiling...It may have been because he had difficulty sleeping between the two girls that Eguchi had a succession of nightmares. There was no thread running through them, but they were disturbingly erotic. In the last of them he came home from his honeymoon to find flowers like red dahlias blooming and waving in such profusion that they almost buried the house. Wondering whether it was the right house, he hesitated to go inside.[23]

The fifth sleeping beauty is the Dreamer, in that she stirs all night beside the Old Man, muttering incomprehensible responses to the figments and nightmares of her mind…and thereby also sends him reeling into rarest, tangled dreams. Thus she is a figure tied to concepts of vision and restlessness.

The Dreamer here allows us to consider a more evolved theory of wish-fulfillment: beyond all analyses linking dreams to the individual unconscious (that which one does not know one truly wants), instead we find a siphoning logic that runs its tubes almost telepathically from one somnambular being to another. The gauntlet; the threading. These red dahlias are not necessarily the assortment of the Old Man's unrealized desires, but just might be the funneling of his companion's desires into the domain of his nightly repose. For what if it is *she* who makes him dream like this (the prime Dreamer)? What if the flowers whose blood-colored outgrowth "almost buried the house" are insinuations, emanations, or projections of the sleeping beauty? Her frenzied turning back and forth upon the bed is therefore a kind of ritual trance or importation-exportation mechanism, one that somehow converts him into pure vessel/receptacle of the woman who "seemed that she was smiling." The smile is all too knowing, fiendish, wickedly clever; it is the prelude to a forced lull (collusion with the unreal).

6. Corpse (dread, prophecy)

He was facing the dark girl. Her body was cold. He started up. She was not breathing. He felt her breast. There was no pulse. He leaped up. He staggered and fell.[24]

Lastly, the sixth sleeping beauty is the Corpse, in that she literally withers beside the Old Man at the story's end, either by malevolent design or accidental overdose to the drug given to her hours before. She breathes her last and turns cold to his despair, a looking glass onto his own approaching fate (wilting icon). Thus she is a figure tied to concepts of dread and prophecy.

In the moments preceding her actual expiration, the Old Man already experiences disgust for her (she is deathly before death). She gives off a pre-emptive foulness; he squirms next to her, avoiding contact. She is at once harbinger and onslaught; she foretells the denied forthcoming; she incarnates decadence, turning fate into flesh that then immediately decomposes.

In this respect, the Corpse plays an oracular or sibylline role; she facilitates an occultic divulgence of the soon-to-come, thus compelling the Old Man to confront certain death before his final demise (virtual euthanasia). An inversion of the starkest order: for death typically arrives too early, making consciousness grasp too late; nevertheless, here consciousness apprehends precisely too early the sheer deathliness deferred to the not-much-later (thought's aftermath). No longer ambush; now only the hanging strain of the already-determined.

Madame

Beyond this, there is the inn's Madame who personifies the Protector, the Instructor, and the Concealer. She synchronously bears both quiet and disquiet, a seer who can tamper with certain laws of heat, sound, and conscience; she guarantees the self-contained ethereality of this location by combining (within herself) the handmaiden's modesty with the empress's sense of aloof dominion; she administers the designated capsules, injections, and anesthetics at their designated moments...and then waits.

1. Protector (calmness, defense)

"Completely out of the question." The woman's face had taken on a muddy pallor, and her shoulders were rigid. "You're really going too far."[25]

The first duty of the Madame is that of the Protector (to safeguard implausible criteria), thus tied to concepts of calmness and defense. The way the Madame drifts in and out of the story's narrative center allows us to ask whether there resides a certain virility within the understated form (the below; the gone-under), and a certain valor among the underwhelming? It is not beyond her to slit the jugular vein of whomever offends the inn's hospitality, for she alone establishes the fair rules of engagement, announcing with "rigid" gravity those allowed and disallowed acts ("going too far"). Hence she is a caretaker in the most forcible sense of the regimen, setting boundaries and organizing all of the event's accessories (more crucial than the event itself): she holds the passcodes, the tablets, the garments, and the ruling logic of all transpirations.

2. Instructor (suggestion, hierarchy)

He was not to do anything in bad taste, the woman of the inn warned old Eguchi. He was not to put his finger into the mouth of the sleeping girl, or try anything else of that sort.[26]

The second duty of the Madame is that of the Instructor (to impart arcane principles), thus tied to concepts of suggestion and hierarchy. Quite simply, the teacher in a seductive zone must negotiate a difficult balance: she must carefully explain the shut doors and ajar doors of potentiality while leaving enough expanse to the guest's imagination as not to spoil the affair's enchantment. The Old Man must therefore be "warned" repeatedly, but in a way that the restriction of certain possibilities only enhances the remaining prospects of sensation, desire, and encounter. She must erect walls that somehow feel permeable, maintain durations that feel timeless, suspending hungers from the all-too-soft hooks of lethargy and narcosis. Hence her most binding words have persuasive effect (the dead-end becomes the opening), sealing a pendulous association between constraint and creativity...and all the while reminding entrants of her superior status in this ill-boding plane, an at once benevolent and merciless disciplinarian of the scales.

3. Concealer (secrecy, anonymity)

"Please. You needn't bother. Go on back to sleep. There is the other girl"...
He heard her dragging the dark girl downstairs.[27]

The third duty of the Madame is that of the Concealer (to cloak unwelcomed variables), thus tied to concepts of secrecy and anonymity. We know nothing of her background, not even her name; she discloses no personal tastes or ambitions and starts philosophical conversations with an air of pure neutrality. What we learn, above all else, is that she enforces the reigning parameters of this place at all costs, and with almost monastic consistency. Her patience is staggering; she sits perpetually ready in nearby hallways, attentive to whatever emergencies or disturbances arise. Though we have no exact indication of what she does in other spaces while the Old Man busies himself, she never falters in her availability, ingenuity, or composure in managing the fluctuations of the inn's magnetic field: at the enticing onset, she executes a pharmaconic task, dwelling expertly in the world of balms, lotions, sedatives, and serums; at the more sullen end of the spectrum, she upholds an occlusive obligation, covering over the destructive underpinnings of this abode and disposing of its obsolete cadavers. Half-water; half-stone. "There is the other girl," she says coolly when a sleeping beauty finally succumbs to lifelessness, disguising the unexpected twist of fortune as if nothing ever happened (for she will erase all fingerprints). No, nothing must stop here; no lingering iota of psyche or maternality; no personal identity to risk compassion, longing, or fear; no ethical universe beyond this iron-clad loyalty to the creed of a single house's exception that begins each twilight and dies at dawn.

Associates, Objects

But I have a ghost here inside me. You have one too.[28]

And there are the Associates, who function as Tempters, Suicides, or Ghosts. There are also the objects that create an intricate backdrop like no other (coupling sloth with nitroglycerin), each a well-inserted artifact of immensely important properties, including: the gate, the key, the blanket, the screen, the cigarette, the toy, the robe, and the pills. And there are the vast acrimonious forces of atmosphere, including the waves, the sea, the snow, the rain, the cold and warmth, the festival, wallpaper, curtains, and the inn's own gauntly-drawn architecture. And perhaps above all else, there are the body parts, each forging its own unique point of intrusion or extrusion, including: the mouth, the teeth, the foot, breast, nose, hair, and skin. Together, these disparate elements forge the base of a far-flung epicenter; together, they propagate the perilous scenario over and again.

Nothing in this place is accidental; everything and everyone serves a delicate nocturnal purpose; they are the essential proselytes of a witching hour, tiptoeing outside the extant to call forth the inexistent session; they are the playing cards or tokens of a shunned gameboard, their agile movements winning rounds, gaining advantages, and collecting pieces for their master Night (which competes only against itself).

Concept Map (of the Inexistent Night; dark figures)

I.
FIGURES

THE SLEEPING BEAUTIES

1. Guide (portal, initiation)
2. Witch (magicality, seduction)
3. Innocent (doubt, manipulation)
4. Recollector (image, return)
5. Dreamer (vision, restlessness)
6. Corpse (dread, prophecy)

THE OLD MAN

1. Watcher (distance, fascination)

2. Deviant (violation, play)

3. Warlord (cruelty, anger)

4. Dying Man (eventuality, surrender)

THE MADAME

1. Protector (calmness, defense)

2. Instructor (suggestion, hierarchy)

3. Concealer (secrecy, anonymity)

THE ASSOCIATES

1. Tempter (rumor, conspiracy)
2. Suicide (disgrace, tranquility)
3. Ghost (scorn, schism)

II.
OBJECTS
(gate) (key) (blanket) (screen) (cigarette)
(robe) (toy) (pills)

III.
ATMOSPHERES
(waves) (sea) (snow) (rain) (cold) (warmth) (festival)
(wallpaper) (curtains) (inn)

IV.
BODY PARTS
(mouth) (teeth) (foot) (breast) (nose)
(skin) (hair)

House of the Sleeping Beauties, photographer: Kurt Van der Elst (from the opera directed by Guy Cassiers, composed by Kris Defoort, and choreographed by Sidi Larbi Cherkaoui, 2009).

Chapter 3

Ascension (dark objects): Prophet's Night; Lunatic's Night; Mystic's Night

Our Prophet had two ascensions, and both occurred in one night.
The Ilkhanid Book of Ascension, anonymous[29]

Lunacy is an incredibly elegant term in that it etymologically weds the concepts of madness and the night's moon (i.e. the lunar cycle). This makes complete sense when we conceive of madness as a giving-way and giving-over of the individual self to an external force (like staring awestruck at a giant white orb), the subordination of subjective identity to something else that demands things from the outside-going-inside. The spellbound, the mesmerized, the aghast: these words begin to scratch the transfixing surface of the lunatic's look. Thus the delusional figure gives license to certain invasive visions; the maniac gives license to certain invasive affects; and the schizophrenic gives license to certain invasive voices. This is what terrifies psychoanalysts and society about all raving figures—their capacity for full self-subjugation before the rushing tides of the faraway (real or imagined)—for which only the child's curiosity and the prophet's sacrificial-volcanic humility provide parallels. Indeed, fairy tales and hagiographies have much in common: themes of departure, miracle, and encounter with implausible creatures/beings that share equally implausible powers.

The medieval Islamic world renders us countless templates linking Night to sacred and profane realms—stories of augury, mantic beings, and vatic utterances in circulation from all sides. From the master storytelling of the *Thousand and One Nights* to myriad Qur'anic *suras* describing God's turbulent relation to obscurity, we can locate a truly pythonic archive of narrative, poetic, and religio-philosophical reflections on nocturnality in this time period. Not to mention that the entire Islamic faith became symbolized (not coincidentally) by the crescent moon — yes, what has often been deemed the Golden Age of Islamic Thought might therefore more accurately be called a Dark Ages of its own, though one of brilliant speculative accomplishments.[30]

From this immense range of pitch-black texts, we will isolate just one radical example for our immediate purposes: the book of the night-journey (*isra'*) and ascension (*mi'raj*). At its most archetypal level, it is a genre devoted to recounting the sky-voyage of the Prophet Mohammad from Mecca to Jerusalem and then upwards into heavenly spheres, filled with supernatural descriptive passages of guardian angels, paradisiac gardens, hell-bound valleys, meteorological orbits, fatal latitudes and meridians, and the gargantuan throne of God itself. And while there have manifested several iconic versions of this ascendant night-journey over the centuries, all with creatively-diverging details therein, including Dante's own *mi'raj*-inspired divine comedy, we will follow here a lesser-known mystical rendition of the tale: written in black ink with Persian calligraphy around the year AD 1286 (during the Ilkhanid Dynasty), with no precise location or author's name given; this elaborate tale will provide us with the necessary visionary particles from which to construct a new theory of the Prophetic Night.[31] Moreover, we will forego traditional entry-points of analysis (i.e. super-ordinant historical factors or theological arguments) by focusing on those often-overlooked features that nonetheless arguably carry the experiential load of the story itself: the objects of the night-journey. So it is that one approaches the heavenly chambers as one would a collector's prized room, basking in wonderment before the Night's things.

Prophecy, Night, Chest

I saw a basin of gold and a gold water pitcher from paradise. Then Gabriel laid me down and split open my chest. He took out several clots of black blood from my heart and threw [them] away...He washed my heart in it and filled it with knowledge, wisdom, and light. He rubbed his wings on me. He put my heart back in its place...My chest returned to what it had been.[32]

First rite of passage (for the night-journey to commence): a high-ranking angel must plunge his hand into the prophet's chest, clench the heart organ, rip it from its cavity, rinse its bloody form in sacred water, and then finally reach back into the split torso to restore its proper placement. A sudden mutilation and healing ritual for which there exists almost no time-lapse between being torn apart and being sewn back together.

This initial encounter with the riven chest establishes two important methodological qualifications for how one reads the entire ascension: (1) that Prophetic Night constitutes a drawbridge to objectionable side-effects, allowing us to undertake fascinating *counter-phenomenologies* where things expand beyond their supposed functionality and meaning to gain multi-potential ability (thus the chest is no longer a site of intimate protection, its sternum and ribcage shielding vital organs, but rather becomes the site of sleek incision-excision); (2) that Prophetic Night represents a third category beyond apophatic mysticism (approaching God through negative statements as to what the deity is not or makes impossible) and cataphatic theology (approaching God through affirmative statements about the deity's attributes or presence). Instead, we are in a more *halluci-phatic* state of explicit, graphic descriptions of properties that are nevertheless previously indescribable (this is why the prophetic figure often faints before divinities

in true revealed form). And both of these conjectural twists—
the *counter-phenomenological* and the *halluci-phatic*—derive
from the chest's being rent asunder and resealed, making us
ask ourselves whether we stand equipped to consider a new
prototype of being: no longer the recognized dualism of unified
being versus divided being, but now the advent of the being-slit-
and-resutured. Patchwork messianism.

Lastly, we can derive a further unconventional assumption
about the night-journey from this abdominal blessing: that
it represents a state of momentary perfection. The prophet
is only temporarily infallible, and the Prophetic Night only
temporarily offered (through angelic vivisection). Against all
typical paradigms of eternity, the ascension constitutes a special
interval, the promise of a single night, nothing more, and with
no hope of further recurrence. Its rarity is therefore paramount:
precious states of a split-second flawlessness never to be
replicated or regained, as long as the shortest duration between
wounding and scarification.

Prophecy, Night, Wing

He saw [Gabriel in his totality] and withstood [this vision],
and he did not faint from seeing him...As the Prophet said,
"I saw Gabriel in the air from the east to the west. The world
was filled by one of his wings, and I saw his wings as white
as pearl. On his head were strands of hair of every colour; his
forehead was like the sun; his feet were like strung pearls;
and some of his feathers were green."[33]

The night-journey is not a predominantly spiritual enterprise,
but rather strictly corporeal from its outset: it does not begin
from the abstract soul but from the throbbing heart, the jeweled
wing, the luminescent forehead, the dappled and polychromatic
hair follicles. Moreover, the angel's fluttering wing in particular

reopens the relational channel between desire and fear—i.e., to fear what we desire and desire what we fear—through ratios monitored by the sensual universe alone.

We discover that the Prophet himself first requests to stare upon the angelic corpus, only to falter and lose consciousness (price of instantaneity). He then awakens and solicits again (note: throughout the night-journey's course, he is occasionally granted second chances, though also often barred from them), and in this subsequent exposure withstands the full force of the wing that spans entire worlds. Still, the vision is not without its frightful consequences.

Prophetic Night hereby enables a new theory of convolution based in the idea of Divinity as Nerve Agent. Specifically, there is almost an identical parallel between the physiological symptoms of nerve agents (sarin, cyclosarin, tabun, soman) and the mystical descriptions of seeing an angel's body: respiratory failure, diaphragm hyperactivity, fainting, pupil constriction, salivation, myoclonic jerks (muscle spasms), cardiac arrest. Both the angelic wing and the nerve agent cause synaptic breakdown and cholinergic crisis; both deliver neuromuscular shock transmitted in aerosol or vaporized forms; both hold their chosen victim captive in a state of poisonous ventilation. The angelic wing is inhaled, thus making the Prophetic Night a kind of strange breathing apparatus.

Prophecy, Night, Steed

Gabriel said, "O Muhammad, rise and sit on this *buraq*." I saw a steed standing on the plain of Safa and Marwa. It was like a horse, smaller than a mule and bigger than a donkey. Its face was like a human's face, and its ears were like the ears of an elephant...Its head was of ruby, its wings of pearl, its rump of coral, its ears of emerald, and its belly of red coral. Its eyes were like glittering stars, and its tail of pearl, and its reins of light.[34]

The night-journey has so far solidified both its induction ceremony and its celestial envoy, but now requires a powerful vehicle to traverse from geographical to cosmological space. Thus marks the arrival of the ascension's steed, a mythic creature from the heavens named *Buraq* (Arabic "lightning") with compound features that range a complex spectrum from animality to humanoid to gemological multiplicities. Alternate versions of the mount include even further machinic, vegetal, or spectral virtues. All in all, these bizarre combinations force us to regard the Prophetic Night as disloyal to the taxonomical purity of creation; rather, it proves beholden to the impure, the bastard, the misceginated, and the half-blood. Buraq's vigor derives from precise adulterations and cross-bred ingredients, the rabid medley of traits/aspects which together stretch the barometers of hybridity, androgeny, and disproportionality.

The amalgamated body of the steed somehow propels it to steer outward and beyond earthly boundaries, its own confusing lineage allowing it an anti-linearity of movement (zig-zagging, levitation, elliptical arcing). The prophetic passenger clings for dear life, as if under electroshock therapy...never teleological progressions, only meteoric spinning and jolting. From this, we can pursue an intriguing theory of Prophetic Night as Universal Banishment: for the celestial is not a homecoming but a breakneck travel elsewhere (ultimate distantiation); it is not a journey-to-the-center but instead an exile-to-the-edge of all things. Heaven as no-man's land; heaven's steed as an empty train nearing the last stop of an abandoned line.

Prophecy, Night, Silk

I passed that place and arrived further. An old hag with an ugly face stood in front of me. She was decorated with many adornments, trimmings, and various silks. She said to me, "O Muhammad, stay so that I can say a word to you." I took only one glance at her and I passed on…That was the world that showed herself ornamented.[35]

At this stage, the night-journey delves into a convincing image/discussion of ornamentality, portraying being-in-the-world itself as a refined practice of seduction, artifice, and cosmetic embellishment. The old-hag world therefore drapes herself in many silks, covering whatever innate ugliness with a supplemental beauty based on optical tricks and enhancements.

But what does this say ultimately of earthly creation? Must not the Prophet eventually return and spread messages to this same intrinsically disgusting plane? Only one of three interpretive options arise: (1) that God's foray into worlding was itself a gross error (the divine hand's misaim); (2) that God enjoys a macabre taste for the grotesque (the divine penchant for building foul things); (3) that in the timeless hierarchy between essence and appearance, God actually favors appearance (the divine ruse of painting cracked surfaces). An aesthetic outlook thereby overrides its theological counterpart, for authenticity is never an a priori possession but rather obtained through the challenging task of effectuation. Can one be innately repulsive and yet still irresistible, or better yet somehow transform repulsion itself into a force of irresistibility? Silk turns the jagged soft; silk wraps the malignant in benign strands, smoothing over disesteemed auras; silk converts degraded rawness into luxuriation, tempting judgment toward overestimation and overvaluation.

Furthermore, can a nocturnal object like silk bestow charismatic power, and does heaven itself consist of such micro-techniques of superficiality? To garnish, dress, gild, or array the original disgrace. Prophetic Night thus upholds the secret axiom of the designer, the seamstress, the architect, the sculptor, the illusionist, the surgeon, and the perfumer: supremacy of the façade over the face (at all costs, and by all false means).

Prophecy, Night, Rock

> I heard a voice, whose intensity caused me to tremble with
> fear...I said, "O Gabriel, what is this terrible sound?" He
> answered, "O Muhammad, know that on that day God
> created hell, a rock slipped from the edge of hell. Until tonight
> it's been falling down. It has reached the bottom of hell just
> now."[36]

Prophetic Night marks the hour of a certain infernal-geological finale, but what does the millennial dropping of this stone foretell beyond itself? This echo of a single petrous fragment surpasses all the worst clichés of psychedelic, out-of-body experiences of a harmonious universe; the flint chip undermines the whole project of totality with its own autocratic finesse. No drug elevates perception here, but rather sensory perception becomes its own narcotic device (night-journey as bad trip), resounding the turmoil behind all firmaments. Incendiary mineral.

The immediate notion to infer is that there exists a sonic register for declension (the acoustics of plummeting things), and that hearing/listening is closely linked to ominous experience. Indeed, omens themselves are often tied to sound (the bell's toll, the wolf's howl, the thunder's rumble), but here we wonder about the role of a netherworld signal amid the procession of a Prophetic Night (does hell also prophesize?). Longevity, depth, the bottom: the pit's conceptual trinity. Is the rock's crashing a mockery, warning, or prediction of some failed hostile takeover? Or if it rings out a culmination rather than a portent, then what unfinished business or unpaid loan does the night-journey resolve at long last? The foreboding; the settlement: ascension haunted throughout by the sound of damnation's crust hitting the cosmic floor.

Prophecy, Night, Cup

Gabriel arrived and offered me three cups..."The die is cast, it's all gone."[37]

The test of three or four cups is a formative event in the eyes of the celestial onlookers, for it measures a certain rarefied type of wisdom/negligence: the ability to choose correctly on others' behalf, without knowing how or why. Water, wine, milk, honey: contents of the four chalices placed before the Prophet on his night-journey (who was told nothing of their symbolic meaning or the examination's stakes). He is then commanded to select according to his "desire," half-passing the trial by drinking milk above other liquids and thus rescuing his community from other terrible fates—water represented a future of drowned followers, wine represented drunken followers, and honey represented lustful followers—but in not draining the milk-filled cup empty is also condemned to having half-deluded members pollute the faith forever. When he quickly petitions to drink the remainder, it is declared too late (note: the being-too-late is an entire philosophical experience with its own exceptional complexity).

With this backdrop established, we must extract some rather subversive conceptual fusions happening in an otherwise sacred experiment, as an all-or-nothing divine verdict hangs in the balance of a lone swallowing-act. For what is the precise criterion by which the night-journeyer arrives at the righteous decision? There is no rational basis to discern the proper cup here, no tradition of theological knowledge or esoteric information from which an illiterate prophetic figure can draw, nor is it some passive surrender to vague faith to determine proper outcomes, nor is there any suggestion of intuitive-experiential awareness (gnosis) to lead the final action. Instead, the prophet is encouraged only to follow his throat's "desire" (opening an entire floodgate to mechanisms of instinct, taste, sensitivity), and consequently is met with a description of the four cups as a kind of dice-throw (opening an equal floodgate to mechanisms of chance, accident, luck).

To feign simplicity: "I always had preferred milk," the Prophet allegedly states.[38] Neither the game's rules nor the game's rewards are made clear until over, thus compelling the practitioner of Prophetic Night to fling his followers' future to a short-lived personal indulgence of thirst (individual whim becoming infinite salvation). Predilection, affinity, partialities of savoring and quenching, the crooked pendulum between liking and likelihood: these are apparently what balance creation's scales for all time to come. Divine justice is a mere casino game, its blessings/curses dispensed via the hazard of four cups...and a razor-thin parting of the lips.

Prophecy, Night, Bird/Sea

I saw birds dwelling in the air. They were eating their daily bread and dying in the air.
Then I passed that place and saw a sea that was floating in the air. Its name was Fate (*qaziya*).[39]

The mid-air death of birds or floating leagues of sea described above point to another of the singular effects of Prophetic Night: the power of suspension (to make life hover). It is what ghosts and shadows do with horrible grace—this hanging, lingering, stillness in open space, the reversal of things that fly or flow into frigid phenomena. Waves meant to transport now cement themselves; food meant to nourish now cramps the beast's stomach. On the one hand, these dangling forms combine conditions of the subject caught-between, at once vertically compressed (between atmospheres) and horizontally imprisoned (between expanses); on the other hand, these dormant forms combine the most extreme manifestations of two dreads,

56

taking to their illogical limit both Sitophobia (the fear of eating anything) and Aquaphobia (the fear of drowning everywhere). Indeed, something above or below has figured out the riddle of fate and fatality's union, and that it rests somehow in the sorcery of undoing rhythm, the drawing of all things into jeopardy of the dead-stop...which might actually just be the acceleration of time to the drastic point of immobility.

Prophecy, Night, Door

I went further, and I saw a throne (*takhti*) set up [in that place]. Adam was sitting upon it. Two doors were open before him: one on the right side, and the other on the left side. When he looked toward the door on the right side, he smiled; and when he looked toward the one on the left, he wept.[40]

The first human (of the garden, the fall) remains inextricably attached to all thematics of shame, defeat, betrayal, and exile. Yet it is the system of opposing doors that catches our critical interest here: for retribution against the human ancestor (Adam) takes the form of everlasting schism. One door stares into heaven, and his eyes flash delighted at the sight of his children there; one door stares into hell, and he grieves through swollen eyelids and wetted eyelashes at the sight of his children there. His purgatorial ordeal does not consist of being denied either paradise or abyss, but rather of being bombarded by both realms simultaneously: the vertigo of the forever-revolving doors, wrenched back and forth until some apocalyptic closure arrives. Prophetic Night thereby trains one to look in two spots at the same time, to walk through two gates concurrently, and to accept the tormented excitement of being in two places at once.

This precursor is both most elected and most vilified, yet the magnetic element here resides in the facial contortions and shifting expressions that correlate to the two swinging doors on either side. The continual oscillation between portals causes a kind of tragicomic dualism to etch itself across the cheeks of Adam; the edges of his mouth turn upward and downward involuntary like the latches and bolts of the doors themselves. He moves between lamenter and euphoriac in rapid succession, just long enough to internalize the respective pangs of self-reproach or pride, and thereby approximates the contradicting Janus-face of pagan worlds (Roman two-faced god of beginnings, duality, transitions, and doorways). The symptomatology of both pantheons is almost identical, making us wonder if we can extend this travesty of emotive confusion to the monotheistic source as well: Does the Creator not withstand a similar conflict, forced to pour perception through the open doors of both perfection and odium? Is omniscience itself not an appalling cascade of images? Is the insistence in Islamic doctrine on the concealed, unseen face of God not a matter of transcendent absence (facelessness) but of profuse dissension, variance, discord, agitation (infinite faces), the divine brow mangled by hyper-reactivity like a rusted double-hinge?

Prophecy, Night, Weapon

Then I saw angels covered with ornaments and with weapons of warriors (*ghaziyan*) made of light. All of them were marching...[41]

The artisanal-allegorical histories of weapons are countless and remarkable, each civilization giving rise to elaborate devices of infliction with their own decorative patterns and technical advantages, but here we are asked to contemplate the more fantastic grades of angelic weaponry. First questions: Do their implements resemble human ammunitions (curvatures of the scimitar, blood-grooves of the dagger), and why are such militaristic angels even required in heavenly domains (threat of siege, invading forces)? Martial law, emergency protocol, vulnerable perimeter, security state: What unnamed rival empire might make necessary the patrols of a cosmic fortress?

We are given a convenient answer later in this same passage of the night-journey/ascension: that they are lithe fighters dispatched by God to aid human warriors in their ongoing struggles. Thus the angelic regiments give surreptitious aid on the battlefields of earthly combat (hidden yet lethal), and are equipped all the while with luminescent blades. The descriptive consequence is twofold: (1) that such celestial details can strike at the speed of light, imperceptibly fast in their violent interventions; (2) that we should hereafter mistrust all radiance, alarmed to learn that most light-formations convey a kind of subtle otherworldly assassination-intent, and that perhaps solarity itself is nothing more than a sharpened spear, knife, or axe.

Prophecy, Night, Tablet

> I saw a tablet (*lawhi*) on his right... He was looking at it with anger... Muhammad asked, "O Gabriel, what is this tablet, what is this tree, and what is this bowl?" He answered, "O Muhammad, on this tablet is a written document (*nuskhat*) of the living creatures who will die this year according to the Guarded Tablet (*al-lawh al-mahfuz*). Azra'il was entrusted with it on the Night of Repentance."[42]

The tablet is what makes the Angel of Death more than just another emissary or ambassador of divine will; rather, the formal inscription of terminal events (and their "guarded" nature) makes him the "entrusted" to a secret awareness of the overall plan. Accordingly, he becomes a true enforcer of the unfolding, from the Night of Genesis to the Night of Repentance to the Night of Armageddon.

But this tablet-bearing takes its apparent toll, for at first we ask ourselves why Death seems overwhelmed by anger. Is it the annoyance of endless, futile supplications of the dying (that they keep pleading)? Is it the ceaselessness of the parade (that they keep coming)? No, it is the tablet itself that rouses anger, for what could have been a maniacally supple gesture of confiscation has now become a rigid function of universal finitude, quantification, and keeping-track (institutionalized record). Accumulation becomes plagued thought, with Azra'il wracked by the sheer anxiety of the inventory, mirroring the addictive transition that all collectors make from pleasure to neurosis. Unrelieving list: to follow strictest orders of eventuality and take every last name unto affliction, without exemption, without playful improvisation (the tablet's demand). Prophetic Night as confrontation with death's incensement, preoccupation, rage.

Prophecy, Night, Hell (Lock, Camphor, Chain, Nail, Drink, Fruit, Head, Neck, Mouth, Tongue, Stomach, Scorpion, River, Valley)

I saw a door of camphor with a lock of gold placed on it... When I looked, the heavens disappeared and a land appeared. I looked, and I saw a man standing there with a dark face, cat eyes, and fire coming out of his mouth.[43]

Hell is an open-air prison: throughout its many descending lairs, we find victims with severed jugulars (Persian *shah-rag*, meaning "king's vein"); we find victims damned to coprophagia (eating of waste) and necrophagia (eating of the dead); we find victims murdered repeatedly in the ways of *sag-marg* ("dog-death") and *zajr-kosh* ("pain-killing"), the former tied to visual humiliation and the latter to physical mutilation. Butchery. Nevertheless, even the night-journey's sulfuric stations are best dissected through their material objects and arrangement of disparate objective forces, allowing us to break down their frameworks of crevasse and brimstone along three separate lines: (1) artifacts of hell; (2) body parts of hell; (3) topographies of hell.

Land of ill-temper; of slow-burn: our first material artifact is that of a door lock (to keep in or keep out?), one varnished with the corpse-washer's and ancient embalmer's favorite substance of camphor (used to douse dead bodies), which confirms an unexpected link between the demonic and the aromachological (mastery of the psychological effects of fragrance). The second material object is the chain, as the Prophet beholds "men and women, fettered in chains and yokes in torment," though we later find a sacred twin to the profane calamity whereby the Prophet describes "that fish on whose back are placed the earths and whose neck is adorned with golden chains."[44] Hence the entire gambit of creation can be classified as an experience of ligatures, cords, and shackles; at either pole of the moral universe, there is only confinement. Thirdly, we find those whose "feet were fastened with fiery nails," thus introducing the nail and its impalement-potential to the mix of grisly circumstances, while the fourth modality incurs the crushing-effect of gravel, rubble, and ore: "stones placed on their heads" and "boulders hanging from the necks."[45] To be pierced by metal spikes or pins is to feel the wrath of interiority; to be pressed-to-death by slabs is to feel the wrath of exteriority. Lastly, infernal punishment moves from solid to liquid techniques (coerced absorption), as some "drink boiling water (*hamim*) and filth (*ghislin*)" while still others have devils "force-feeding them Zaqqum [fruits]."[46] Each crucible partakes of its own unbearable dimension (scalding, retching, clenching). One shrieks at the first; one gags at the second; one chokes on the third...though all pay their tribute to the inconsumable (gorging nevertheless, against the will).

From the material artifacts of hell, we shift focus to the

beleaguered organs of its denizens. While the head, neck, and spinal areas are immediately implicated through acts of weighing-down, the mouth and tongue then become instrumental players as well in verses where "demons were placing fiery bits of corpses into their mouths" and "putting rotten meat into their mouths," or where "tongues were hanging to their navels" and "ichor was dripping from their tongues."[47] Whereas feeding on decomposed tissue constitutes a hygienic threat, and feeding on dead flesh an obscene violation, ichor interestingly refers both to the mythic substance that runs in the veins of pagan gods and the putrid discharge that oozes from fresh wounds (does divinity possess its own laws of festering, infection, and decay?). Beyond this, we reach the condemned stomach, with certain bellies "stretched out to the size of several mountains" and others "turning on fiery millstones" or with "intestines coming out from their posteriors."[48] These methods of expansion, roasting, or purging all bend toward an inability to self-contain Being; they are meant to precipitate the nonstop leaking of the inward outward.

Still, the wondrous repercussion of all these bodily disjointments is the emergence of a grand scorpion to poke the hell-dwellers, a creature whose incredible anatomy combines and magnifies each aforementioned fracture of appendages: for "every scorpion was the size of several camels, and every scorpion had seventy tails, and every tail had seventy joints, and for every joint there was a sack of poison."[49] The beast's skeletal system is rendered gigantic and multitudinous: ideal killing-machine; the back-biter; conglomeration of miscellaneous fatal pinpoints and poisoned tips; death by a thousand stings (though undying).

The final element to scrutinize in the night-journey's hellscape relates to its vivid orchestration of space, landscape, terrain, position, and climate. Carcasses are dragged through snake-filled meadows or into torture shacks with cat-eyed wardens standing watch, forming caravans of the discredited, sprained, and beaten. This notwithstanding, the assorted vistas of river and valley in the text allow us to best understand the unnatural architectonics of perdition: in one direction, a "river of bile, blood, worms, and fire...boiling together, putrid and revolting" alongside another "black and rippled with fire... growling at itself with clamour and terror"; in a second direction, valleys for which "they say that the name of the valley is Vayl (affliction), and the other is called Sijin (captive) and the Lowest of the Low."[50] The waterways churn like the potions of wizards, mixing gory things and streaming contamination upon bodies therein with their own doses of base materialism; the ravines, however, follow a more cryptic route with titles that subsume sophisticated concepts (affliction, captivity, abject lowness), avenging themselves against the disobedient in the format of abstract art or experimental cuisine that demand a certain oblique consciousness from the participant. In either instance, we have lost the orientational sense of north, south, east, or west...like the temperatures also in incessant flux...verifying that ascension includes descent (not to mention spiraling, crisscrossing, teleportation, and sailing).

Prophecy, Night, Chant

I saw their entire stature to be entirely face, with no hands or feet...singing God's praises in delight and in song. This delight did not resemble another, and that angel did not resemble this one. They were all weeping from their awe of God...[51]

Prophetic Night emerges from its third-degree blazing to rediscover the Kingdom once more, but perhaps most shocking is that the physiognomy of the first angels proves almost identical to that of the underworld scorpions. They are multi-headed, multi-faced, multi-mouthed, multi-tongued, and multi-lingual in their collective chant; moreover, they are comprised exclusively of visage (rows of amputated craniums engaged in song). All this notwithstanding, the most significant detail is that of their non-resemblance to one another, each angelic larynx performing its own sound overture in whatever atonal, non-melodious note. Hive-mind, but with sectarian blare: all that matters is the singularity of each vocal chord's "delight," producing an image of the heavens as non-harmonic, anarchic, and cacophonous. Divinity as non-musical, but rather Noise.

Nor is it only the bodiless angelic choir that vibrates into dissonance, but also the prophetic listener himself. Thus he states: "The seven parts of my body became organs of hearing, and hearing from all six directions. I heard from the inside what I heard from the outside; I heard from the right what I heard from the left; and I heard from below what I heard from above."[52] Prophetic Night as pure schizophrenic audition.

Prophecy, Night, Element (Wind, Rain, Froth)

Every day an angel touches Kawthar [paradise's main river] with his wing, pulls it away, lifts its froth, and scatters it. Thousands upon thousands of drops drip down. From every drop, God most High creates an angel.[53]

Before attending to the above passage, one can start a discussion of the night-journey's elementality by noting the several winds that are compartmentalized according to philosophical labels. First there is "the wind of barrenness (rih al-'aqim)," then the wind that blows throughout "the placeless realm," and finally "the wind of mercy (bad-i rahmat)."[54] Upon closer examination, these wind-types all deal with a particular condition of absence, each occupying its own spot in the overall taxonomies of ruin and chasm: the barren wind speaks to the loss of futurity, vitality, or hope; the placeless wind speaks to the loss of territoriality, identity, or groundedness; the merciful wind speaks to the previous committal of offense, and therefore to the loss of innocence, purity, or sanctity. But why would such criminal winds permeate the heavenly ranks, since each is predicated on varying forms of imperfection, gap, or lack? Are the upper floors incomplete, the hereafter riddled with defaults and lapses galore? Does it not suggest that the embryonic defects of life are indeed hereditary, and that the whirling flaws and fissures of existence gust skyward as well? God's lair as without fullness, nor immune to bad cyclones.

The next elemental characteristic pertains to the rains, and to the "angels of rain" whose "faces were like the full moon."[55] At the helm of this entire legion is the archangel Michael, who when asked by the prophetic figure to explain his name's etymology responds as follows: "Because they put me in charge (*muwakkal*) of rain. Not a drop of rain falls on earth without being weighed on my scale."[56] An amazing image of duty: to measure the consecutive densities of each droplet prior to any signs of torrent, downpour, or cloudburst. But why such senseless exactitude, devoting titanic expenditures of energy to tasks of trivial computation? Is all predestination based on absurd analysis, calibrating every ridiculous sprinkling and minor climatological event? Why employ the angel whose reputation extends to victoriously battling Satan for such tiny meteorological inspections, or are these two acts somehow mutually necessary functions (the epic will and the infinitesimal will)?

However, the most gripping elemental production occurs in the description of angel creation itself: namely, that God presumably entrusts this process to a ritual practice carried out by an intermediary river-angel, one who spawns his brothers/ sisters through nothing more than scattered froth. A kind of holy parthenogenesis (reproduction without fertilizing partner), usually reserved in nature for odd plants, insects, amphibians, or reptiles. Yet the integrant of froth is what captures interest here: For what does it mean to delegate the arch-guardians' origination to flaking or dripping matter? Their cores are spawned by incidental, falling substances; their inceptions depend on the delicately random spreading of globules. Replication becomes a matter of foam, spray, spindrift; species-being as neither evolutionary nor sequential, but rather born of effervescent bubbles and air particles.

Prophecy, Night, Veil

I saw the guardian of paradise with angels. There were thousands upon thousands of veils on their moon-like faces...[57]

We fall along another heavenly slope to find innumerable veiled angels. The veil is an intriguing receptacle of competing backstories, for it usually accompanies states of either shame, conspiracy, or superiority. The leper (of humiliated countenances); the bandit (of covert missions); the royal house (of elite standing). Thus it is not logically problematic that the night-journey encounters both galleries of self-covering demonic beings and manors of self-shrouding angelic beings, including even a divinity itself that wears "the veil of Majesty (*hijab-i kibriya*)."[58] Yes, the sovereign also shades itself, beclouding and camouflaging beyond the heaven's balconies, supposedly for reasons of transcendent invisibility but perhaps for the other two aforementioned rationales of veiling as well: on the one hand, that the Creator dissimulates out of some mortification or contempt; on the other hand, that the Creator self-eclipses and blindfolds worlds out of some pending treachery or ulterior motive. So it is that a single garment's fibers can hold entire universes of coveting and scandal.

Let us juxtapose this tactile impact of the veil against the archangel Gabriel about whose name the text claims: "They call Gabriel 'Gabriel' because he oversees the sinking into the ground (*khasf*) and the disfiguration of features (*maskh*) of God's enemies."[59] There is some parallel already to veiling with respect to his controlling forms of submergence and the dramatic altering of the face (creating a mask of lesions); or stated otherwise, he collapses the dialectics of the inside and the outside by making spiritual traitors wear something conspicuous, pronounced, and glaring. Sin emblazoned; Cain's marked forehead; the veil that makes now-unveilable ones.

For the record, the Old Testament references Gabriel as the "man in linen", and Islamic thought only enhances his ethereal status by appointing him the angel of revelation, consolation, and physical splendor. He therefore generally oversees the provinces of tender acts (as confidante). But here he takes his place at the helm of gashing, deformity, and defacement. Is it because cosmic cruelty is not actually a brute-force crude practice, but rather an ever-refined sensitivity (gentle mastery of the fingers)? Is each abrasion a fine-spun, satin maneuver? Is the angel's cutting of the enemy's wrist or heretic's gumline akin to the tailor's rigorous cutting of cloth? If so, then it would make sense to leave such cultivated responsibilities of live burial and knife-play in only the softest, impeccable hands.

Prophecy, Night, House/Tree

They call it the Lote Tree of the Limit because the highest degree of the spirits of the prophets and martyrs is located there.[60]

The house and the tree are things that normally stand strong, but Prophetic Night is a time of great abnormality. The upright turns upside-down; structures that once held together (crumbling only before deluges, hurricanes, or earthquakes) now fall into anomalous disarray. Hence we arrive at the worn threshold of The Frequented House (*al-bayt al-ma'mur*): the edifice encloses a certain solemnity, but the adjective "frequented" hints at an alternative reading of it as an abused, trampled site (the brothel, the tavern, the caravanserai).[61] One pictures dilapidated walls, frayed velvet curtains, and tiles weathered by excessive footsteps; the squatter's haven or tenement building in the heart of the divine metropolis. No more dwelling; only infestation.

The Lote Tree of the Limit is also based upon a riveting principle: that of sacrificial nurturing (watered with the martyrs' blood). Its tangled roots feed off the harassment of this special lot; its low-hanging branches are restored by their carrion-offerings, thus revisiting the primeval religious paradox of enlivening-through-fatality. We are told earlier that the Angel of Death never smiles until Judgment, for Death is created as punishment, but here we find the lone exception by which it becomes pure gift (as serum). For the martyr inspires; the martyr regenerates; the martyr quickens creation's pulse; the martyr makes healthy by going-rancid. In one world, a body spills its agony; in another world, the forest grows.

Prophecy, Night, Ink

He made one drop of the pen's substance fall into the mouth of the Prophet. The knowledge of the first and the last was acquired by his heart. After that, they never asked him something which he could not answer.[62]

Prophetic Night transmits its most secluded, occult knowledge via the trachea. Thus the prophet-journeyer is told to tilt his head back and allow God to pour whatever pigments, dyes, and resins into his open windpipe. This ingestion of ink is a supra-epistemological transfer (to grasp the arcane), allowing familiarity with both the primordial unknown and the future unknown. From the immemorial to the doomsday hour, the ink-stained bloodstream carries/solves all riddles of omniscience. But the question remains: How does such knowledge of the first and last not result in total nihilistic paralysis (the stalemate), gripping all mental exercises in the vise of standstill? Furthermore, does it not make the prophetic figure the target of continual interrogation, always facing the awful pressure of the question, the awful pressure of the answer, on the eve of infinite inquest, before the desperate crowds, his eyes becoming mirror pools of human curiosity and doubt, his voice a cure to the ambiguity of all overarching things? Does the end of consciousness's ambivalence mark the beginning of its radical indifference? Does this all-enveloping catechism (written in eternal ink) not make creation, Creator, and the created intolerable to mind?

Prophecy, Night, Houri (Crown, Bone)

Faces like *houris* without souls grow from its brinks. The believer looks at them and his desire for them enters his heart. At that instant, a soul enters that face, and its head is adorned with a crown and its body with a garment. It stands up before the paradise-dweller.[63]

The houris constitute legendary figures in Islamic iconography: they are desire personified—beautiful, seductive, eternally youthful, without bodily secretions, always plural—given as ideal rewards to believers in the afterlife. In fact, they are overcompensations (samples of the divine's surplus generosity), and are said to enchant through contrast, as evidenced by their shockingly black pupils set within shockingly white eyeballs. To paraphrase the night-journey's author, their showing of a single fingernail has the ability to turn dark night into light, just as the untangling of a single strand of hair turns the earth's soil into musk and the letting fall of a single drop of their saliva turns ocean water sweet. They are therefore faultless companions-in-bliss; they are the baubles of projected yearning, such transparent reflections of fantasy that even "their bone marrow is visible."[64] Additionally, the coronation described above happens only amid the realization of the other's wish, their crowns forged from secret and private appetites (of the voyeur). In this respect, they occupy a third sliver between the metaphysical (no native soul) and the physical (no inborn need), neither purely apostolic nor purely fanciful but of something closer to technics (automation). They are harvested simulacra (unbothered), impersonators of spontaneous urges; their opiate gazes are mere alloys. The barely-hypostatized, they evince lust in all its radical hollowness, the figurines of a meaningless dei-erotics made for partisans. The houris are incorruptible because they exemplify every hedonistic corruption; they remain virginal because they are constantly overtaken. Such is the outermost vision of materiality offered by Prophetic Night: to meet the living plaything (absolute objectification of being).

Prophecy, Night, Throne

Then I passed that place until I reached a dark sea. In it, I saw silent angels that were headless and motionless…They are the spiritual angels, the chamberlains of God's throne.[65]

Asceticism taken to its conceivable brink: to resemble the frightful chamberlains in the above excerpt (headless, motionless, silent), troubling as a wax museum or sculpture garden at night. And then there are the eight throne-carriers, united by their single ominous incantation: "*Praise be to You, the throne knows not where You are.*"[66] This is a terrifying line of poetic-mystical genius: let us sift through all the byzantine descriptions of pedestals, angelic tears, lavender and saffron flowers (all important objects of the Prophetic Night) to ask why God's throne cannot locate its host. It is an abhorrent situation, this vacated regal chair that screams for its master, leading us to ask after the potential causes of such cosmic puzzlement: (1) that this God sometimes flees (runaway divinity), taking leave of his realms to entertain nomadic horizons; (2) that the throne's location is itself a terra incognita, thus confounding spatial understanding and making God undetectable; (3) that either God, the throne, or both are kinetomaniacal forces (always in compulsive movement), gyrating along their own axes and thus interminably missing one another; (4) that divine radiance is itself a form of astigmatism or retinal tearing, thereby leaving the entire perceptual order in fog, daze, astonishment. "I suspected that the people of this world and that world had died," the Prophet confesses in anguish/hysteria. Such is the great knot and thorn of reaching the Throne (akin to derangement).

Epilogue: The Usurper's Night

Bāyazīd compares himself to God, claims the praise of angels in God's stead, turns the direction of prayer (*qebla*) from God to himself, and declares that the Ka'ba walks around him... He is no longer creature and servant of God: "They are all my creatures except you"; "All humans are my servants except you". Instead he becomes God's rival, finding God's throne empty and ascending it in recognition of his own true being: "I am I and thus am 'I'", Bāyazīd claims to be without beginning or end...without morning or evening. God takes second place to him: He replies to the muezzin's call "God is great!" with the words "I am greater!"..., turning the Koranic words "Surely, thy Lord's grasp is firm" (85:12) into "By my life, my grasp is firmer than His" and exclaiming "Moses desired to see God; I do not desire to see God; He desires to see me"...[and] "I am I; there is no God but I; so worship me!"[67]

The well-designed images of the night-journey (the deep-sleeping city, the Prophet's head engulfed in flames, the cartographical layerings of ethers) remind me of a certain spectacle from years ago. There were two professional fighters, both champions in their respective weight classes, talking at an event staged before their actual bout. On the one side, an arrogant conqueror-type who ranted and raved about his prowess, literally pronouncing himself a god among gods at the podium; on the other side, a humble religious figure who saw combat as a personal duty to his prophetic patron, offended by his opponent's pretensions and vowing to chasten with elbows, knees, and chokeholds. The megalomaniac contra the servant. Who holds the advantage in the martial hour? Fiendish confidence (becoming-exalted) or fanatical modesty (becoming-instrument)? The fight never happened in the end, no doctrines avenged or complexes vindicated...but the question remains as to which theo-savant prevails.

The above selection showcases a rare alternative to the Prophetic Night, taken from a different text and author, wherein the medieval Sufi mystic Bayazid Bastami claimed his own nocturnal passage across the skies. The result is a freakish turn of the scales: for the mystic's arrival in heaven leads him to assert his equality and then supersession of the divine Creator, forcing the angelic companies to face him, demanding that prayer and circumambulation realign their trajectories around his new center, climbing the vacant throne of God and commanding superior rites of worship from all beings. Challenger; emergent competitor; mad usurper. Ascension here is no longer merely a semi-performative consideration of the pre-existent but rather an existential call to rivalry of the ultimate, and moreover it consists of an almost unthinkable blending of the two conditions described earlier: namely, the fusion of extreme conceit and extreme self-effacement into a perfect anchor/pedal of the will. And it can happen only at Night, under whose obsidian mantle the paradox of ultra-embodiment (incarnating everything and nothing) takes hold.

Concept Map (of the Ascendant Night; dark objects)

Prophet

chest
wing
steed
silk
rock
cup
bird, sea
door
weapon
tablet
hell (lock, camphor, chain, nail, drink, fruit, head, neck, mouth,
tongue, stomach, scorpion, river, valley)
chant
element (wind, rain, froth)
veil
house, tree
ink
houri (crown, bone)
throne

Usurper

Ascent of Muhammad to Heaven (ca. 1539-1543), ascribed to
Sultan Muhammad. From the *Khamseh of Nizami*.

Chapter 4

Apotheosis (dark concepts): Idol's Night; Pagan's Night; Master's Night

There is a mistaken approach to the divinity cults of ancient worlds: namely, to perceive these deities as abstract embodiments of archetypal human experiences. In this interpretive paradigm, the early gods symbolically represent either repressed internal wishes or complicated external phenomena faced by the half-unconscious, half-knowing subject. But what if this equivalence is entirely wrong? What if these far-reaching divinities are the first signposts of an extra-human imaginary, allowing consciousness to trespass beyond itself, into the realm of unlikely possibility, through new conceptual permutations? What if these retrieved stone faces, often disfigured or beastly or simply unthinkable, have nothing to do with self-reflection yet instead allow thought an excuse for immanent trespass, manifesting the other side of vision's limit? Divine horror/beauty as the first beyond.

Futuristic projections (in literature, theology, visual art) often describe worlds of abiding nocturnality. With the invention of electricity 2 centuries ago, there was a similar optical paranoia that the future would look like perpetual darkness, a fear brought on by the introduction of artificial light into modern cities. Somehow the nineteenth-century's illumination of the metropolis by streetlamps seemed like a diabolical looking glass onto a coming age where no sun or dawn could exist again. All radiance thereafter would become simulated, holographic, fluorescent; false incandescence (alienating glow of the halogen bulb).

But the ancients also shared this paranoiac view of time, which is why their darkness-bound gods and goddesses are nothing less than vital realizations of the demented mind.

76

Night as outliers' stage, both hideous and enthralling; Night as idol's case, with its figurines of mutated arms wielding mallets, hatchets, and cleavers. Their statues are not motivated by standard monumentalizations of the Creator (glorification, idealization) but rather by the counter-monumentalities of the miscreant (tied to suspicion, intimidation, monstrous worship). The night-gods are curious, erratic, not necessarily meant to be.

These upper and lower actors are indeed concepts, but never archetypes. They blossom into lurid quadrants of thought for which there is no solidity (only wading). Nor is there any legitimate political order that follows such night-deities (no chancellors, dynasties, judges), nor any proper priesthood to sermonize or codify rites. There is only the cult leader, whose charismatic powers suffice to bring our fears to life (the nominee, the clairvoyant, the master).

Babylonian Night: Silence, Injustice, Divination

The princes are closely guarded,
The locking-bolts lowered, the locking rings placed,
(Though previously) noisy, the people are silent,
(Though previously) open, the doors are locked.
Babylonian Prayer to the Gods of Night[68]

The Babylonian Prayer to the Gods of Night is a perfect entrance into our claim of conceptual confusion in that it starts already from a suggestion of reversal. Irreproachable authorities (the princes) are now suddenly vulnerable, requiring excess protection; impregnable structures (palaces, temples) are now suddenly breachable, requiring excess fortification; clamorous cultures are suddenly hushed; all portals, gates, and entryways are suddenly closed off. Whatever is supposed to happen—the daily order—is being overturned by the indomitable pressure of Night. Meaning is no longer safe; thinking is not safe; Being is not safe. The great concepts are in disorder.

There are two things to discern quickly from the opening passage of this descriptive scene: (1) that nightfall hosts certain unnamed agents who must actively react to this transition, guarding and locking all sacred spaces; (2) that nightfall hosts certain unnamed agents who must actively break all promises, guarantees, hierarchies, barriers, and vows. The Word (of law, belief, right) is suspended under this state of nocturnal exemption; nothing is honored anymore. Damage can therefore be done to immutable things: on the one side, there are those sworn to preserve regimes through such long nights of potential violence; on the other side, there are those who take their chances at this narrow window to violation. Is it that the elite become embattled while the wretched become predatory (revolutionary inversion), or more interestingly that Night brings forth unknown denominations, non-related pedigrees, and radically-extraneous swarms? Are they ravishing or abject configurations, liberating or merciless, or both simultaneously? We are not even clear on the exact typologies that threaten this civilization's border-walls: human (traitors, pirates, cutthroats), inhuman (monsters, aliens, divinities), natural (earthquakes, cyclones, tidal waves), or magical (spells, curses, destinies). All we know is that the expected world has given way to a trapeze-act of cirque-like alternation.

> The gods of the land (and) the goddesses of the land,
> Shamash, Sin, Adad and Ishtar
> Have entered into the lap of heaven.
> They do not render judgment, they do not decide a case.
> The night is veiled.
> The palace, its chapel, the cella are obscured.
> The traveler invokes god, but the one (who offers) a decision remains
>   asleep.
> The judge of truth, father of the impoverished girl,

Shamash has entered his cella [69]

Spatial juxtaposition 1: "the land" versus "the lap" (surface versus depth), for which the latter posits a site of the gods' infantilization (do they become helpless, childlike again?) or resting (do they enter hibernation, idleness?). Spatial juxtaposition 2: "the traveler" versus "the cella" (exposure versus withdrawal), for which the latter posits the inaccessible site of a sanctuary or temple's inner chamber but also bears etymological resemblance to the prisoner's cell, house's cellar, and cellular level of the body. Thus the apparent world gets thrown into chasms; the inquirer finds no answer awaiting, and the searcher finds no destination reached. Rather, we are in something like *the oubliette* (from the French *oublier*, literally "forgetting" though meaning a dungeon structure with only a single above-head trapdoor). And what happens when all metaphysics descends into such secret vaults, or when gods themselves go sleeping in faraway oubliettes?

Not all celestial forces retreat into the cella, though: hence we must effectively isolate those gods (and by extension concepts) that become obsolete in the face of the Night's obscurity. First there is Shamash, Babylonian-Akkadian sun-god affiliated with justice and righteousness (his two ministers), bearded and long-armed, symbolized by solar disks or radiant four-pointed stars, often carrying a panther-headed scimitar or notched dagger and surrounded by human-headed bulls in ancient iconography. He governs universes on horseback or chariot and presumably inscribes the first legal codes for human civilization, at times represented heroically as a light-bearing conqueror of Night or said to undertake only a restricted function as judge of the underworld during nocturnal hours. A protector of the dead and of the living (merchants, travelers, kings), enforcer of societal warmth and equity. But Shamash has fallen unconscious in this prayer, his irrelevance signaling the absence of fairness, the blurring of omniscience, the delay of verdict, and the aimlessness of quest. In their place, we must assume that opposing or third-degree concepts are then set loose to fulfill their possibilities: bare injustice or amorality filling the void of justice; retroactive vision or blindness to fill the void of divination; non-judgment, random decree, or mal-decision to fill the void of reckoning; wandering, detour, or stillness to fill the void of odyssey. And what happens to our stories when the journey loses its archetypal guarantor, or when the all-seeing shuts its eyes?[70]

Next there is Sin, the Euphrates valley moon-god, patron deity of the city of Ur, father of the sun-god Shamash and Ishtar with whom he forms the astral triad, protector of herders, of the reeds and marshlands, symbolized by a crescent shaped from bull's horns, portrayed as old boatman or cowherd astride a winged bull, tied numerologically to 30 (the lunar month) and often prayed to for fertility and the relieving of birthing pains. In ancient tablets, the moon-god Sin is also known as "he whose heart cannot be read" and who "could see farther than all the gods." Thus we come upon two incredibly significant concepts at work within the deity's power-set: enigma and futurity. But Sin too has gone beneath, into the folds or navel of a certain somnolence, which means we no longer have access to the wisdom of the esoteric/hidden or of the remote/forthcoming; both epistemic and temporal distances are extended into irreconcilability. In their place, we might assume that the guess inhabits the failure of future-telling, and that the many branches of nonsense pervade the failure of the enigma's solution. The radical unknowing of all things forward and backward, upward and downward, and with this the potential disbanding of the herd and the malfunction of reproducibility. And what happens when the crescent moon becomes a dull-blade instrument?

Adad, storm-god and rain-god, originally brought forth by the Amorites, known alternatively as "The Thunderer," often depicted with headdress or horned helmet and lightning spear in hand, symbolized by the lion-dragon or cypress tree, tasked as inspector of cosmological space, deity of rage and temperamental fluctuations, wavering always between benevolence (seasonal rains for harvest) and havoc (floods that destroy crops), married to the goddess of grain yet known for fearful lashings against the land. The absence of Adad (monitor of wells and canals) in our nocturnal prayer therefore brings with it a conceptual unfolding of desolating proportions (those of the dry spell): famine, drought, starvation. Night as starkest finitude; pastoral life turns murderous at dark; the loss of divine anger and the hurricane presumes an age of wanting (weatherlessness). Hereafter hunger, thirst, and survival become the only prime movers; all existence concerns the simple matter of "whatever is left" (scavenging, hoarding, collecting scraps). Let us take two related words to heart, then: *alluvion* ("the wash or flow of water against a shore") and *alluvium* ("a deposit of clay, silt, sand, and gravel left by flowing streams in a river valley or delta"). A causal theory of inundation and detritus to be extended to the theo-terrestrial plane, especially amid now-plantless worlds: For what happens when the storm-god retracts the rain showers (as nothing grows), and residuum alone is left to control the universe?

Last in this sequence is the feminine Ishtar, goddess of the planet Venus, evening and morning star, deity of both sexual desire and warfare, typically depicted nude or with open cape, draped in dark reds and azure blues, weapons strapped across her back, never maternal but always seductively young and promiscuous, guardian of prostitutes, drunkards, and pleasure-seekers, her emblems of the storage gates, rosette, or circular rays found throughout brothels, bathhouses, and taverns across the ancient world. There are even stories of her underworld migration, gradually removing pieces of clothing and jewelry while passing through each level of the Sumerian *Kur* (dismal cavern and shaded mirror-plane of earthly existence). Thus "she evolved into a more complex character, surrounded in myth by death and disaster, a goddess of contradictory connotations and forces — fire and fire-quenching, rejoicing and tears, fair play and enmity."[71] Ishtar as arch-mistress of all sensual and militaristic arts, wielding the aggressive and alluring sensitivities of both realms, and yet the Babylonian Prayer to the Gods of Night strategically suspends her interventions as well. Hence what concepts fill the otherwise intimate voids of both lust and battle? Absolute solitude? A nightside world where nothing ever touches? Or also imagine that the deity's spheres of action remain (sex, war), though with their accompanying passions drained; imagine that all emotional craving, satisfaction, or glory were erased from the experiential strata, leaving only an executioner's stony, anonymous stare and blade. Sensation still abounds, but within total coldness; bodies are still immersed in complex choreographies of entanglement, but driven only by some bleak code of infliction. And what happens when once-sublime coordinations now pass through utmost vacant eyes, and when the pale force of neutrality alone controls the scales of love and hate?

(Side-Note: In the Babylonian Talmud, there appear references to a night-demon named Lillith (derived from the Akkadian *lilitu*, meaning "evening creature, specter, or monster"), known for sexual libidinousness, driving infertile women mad, and kidnapping sleeping children from their beds. Later in Jewish mythology and mystical circles, this nocturnal figure of Lillith is re-interpreted as Adam's first wife in the garden, created from the same dust (as opposed to Eve's association with her husband's ribcage) and therefore refusing submissiveness to her masculine partner. Instead, she betrays him by mating with Samael, the archangel of death, his name meaning "Venom of God," "Poison of God," or "Blindness of God," his titles being the seducer, the accuser, and the destroyer, and their erotic bond is what gives rise to the first demonic race.)[72]

The great ones, the gods of the night,
Bright Girra,
Warrior Erra,
The Bow, the Yoke,
Orion, the Furious Serpent,
The Wagon, the Goat,
The Bison, the Horned Serpent [73]

According to the Babylonian cosmology, Night requires gods capable of abomination (carriers of nocturnal will): these are the grand backstab-artists, the divinities of an abhorrent heritage. Still, an unmentioned name looms in the back pages of this anti-circadian taxonomy: Tiamat, primordial goddess of the salt sea, darkness, chaos, and creation. She is a paradoxical creature from the time of permanent nightfall: a destroyer-deity and yet whose sliced body parts form the heavens and earth; at once represented as unconscious, reckless annihilation and yet also holding diabolical intelligence; bathed in eternal blackness and yet known as "The Glistening One." She is the inadvert mother, a sea serpent from whom the first generation of gods is spawned (in a watery cosmos), though also the first demonic hordes, and whose shaking scales induce the originary maelstroms of existence.

It is by the assertive command of the primeval (eve without day, darkness before light) that the gods of Night issue forth. Most of the above-listed entities are non-identitarian: they are unshackled from the elaborate mythological narratives and symbolic functions of the former deities and instead recognized by their tangible outlines as actual constellations in the night sky. They are visually self-evident by their silhouettes and illuminations, and in place of anthropomorphic reductions are related to the more expansive domains of animality, vehicles, and objects; rather than seeking archetypal meaning, these gods emanate from a perceptual faculty closer to the child's imagination of cloud-shapes (thus apparent resemblance overthrows metaphorical abstraction).

This notwithstanding, there are two specific gods noted at the outset who merit distinction: Girra and Erra. In the first instance (Girra), we stand before a night-god of fire and mercurial light, host to forges, kilns, and smelting blocks, but with three crucial pyrotechnic qualifications: (1) that his fire has primarily technical deployments, as the patron deity of metallurgy and masonry (followers: blacksmiths, ironsmiths, bricklayers); (2) that he has virtually no discovered human iconography (escaping personification), but whose cult sites are littered with the sole emblem of the torch throughout; (3) that he is feared as the source of conflagration, runaway flames, and burning fields. Thus we have a wondrous conceptual collusion at work here: on the one hand, presumed divine forces are falling from their transcendent exclusivity to become concretized forms of labor, visceral expenditure, and artisanal craft (birth of the guilds); on the other hand, this new world of constructive exertion and ingenuity is coupled with a keen awareness of the dystopian potentials of technological invention. This is why Girra is the figure of wicked logos (undoing words), with a "vastness of mind" inscrutable to all other gods: he senses that the house can burn; the city can burn; the entire universe can burn down (to pull levers or switches of macrocosmic ignition). Outside of the pathetic dialectics of metaphysical orthodoxy and humanist ideology—the two dominant phases of historical experience— we have a non-metaphysical and equally non-humanist devotion to the artificer, the handle, and the apparatus above all else. Thus the torch's aesthetic prevalence across Girra's temple walls signals another important facet of Night: that it supplants worship of a being (theo-ontology) with exaltation of an implement (the master's delirium) and the dream of apocalyptic risk (the master's temptation).

In equal fashion, the second listed god in our night-sequence places us before its own dangerous phenomena: Erra, god of plague, of neo-Assyrian origins, pleaded to in desperation on amulet stones and in warding texts, whose name derives etymologically from "charred" or "scorched earth" and whose epithet is "lord who prowls by night." He is the bringer of famine and pestilence, though also protector of hunters, two facts that allow us a conceptual fusion along the following axis: that to engage this leader of the Terrible Seven, one must abandon all viewpoints of outbreak and scourge as purely impulsive or indiscriminate action (ravaging) and instead begin studying a kind of cosmic ballistics (scientific field of mechanics concerned with the launching, propulsion, flight, and effect of projectiles). Pandemic years thereby become an affair of being-shot-through; calamitous time is hereafter gauged through careful attention to trajectory and impact, akin to avalanche or meteoric crashing and to the ever-present possibility of ricochet. Note that the star grouping of The Bow is enlisted directly after Erra's name, for there is a sort of rash archery associated with both nocturnality and contagion.

Is it any wonder, then, that the three aforementioned deities (Tiamat, Girra, Erra) are later complemented in our night-prayer by the "furious" snakes and dragons of constellations? If fury itself is nothing less than the very affective definition of bound-lessness-within-precision, precision-within-boundlessness, then this realization hands Night's dominion over to a new triptych of concepts and their counter-archetypal keepers: paradox (the beast); instrumentality (the builder); unleashing (the despoiler).

May they stand by so that,
In the extispicy I am performing,
In the lamb I am offering,
You may place the truth.[74]

(Side-Story: Let us transcribe here an old tale recounted by my wife's mother, a strange nocturnal encounter that happened to her father in the villages bordering the Iranian salt desert nearly 100 years ago. One night, the story goes, his family was hosting guests and thus told their eldest son to ride on horseback to some nearby opium fields and bring back poppy petals/shavings for those gathered to smoke. On his way back, however, he passed a shrine's cemetery and was startled by the distant glow of a light shining ominously from an empty grave (there was no electricity in such regions at the time). He dismounted and neared the open hole to discover a large candle fastened to a piece of broken wood and the fatty tail of a sheep that was dripping its contents below. As the long wick of the candle burned, the meat had melted down to a single kilogram. It was the vessel of a death-spell, the name of someone attached to its progressive dwindling, their life-span conceivably ebbing drop by drop alongside the cursed lamb's flesh (the final drop implying a fatal outcome). According to the account, her father quickly extinguished the flame out of fright, halting the expiration process, and rode away into the night haunted by his detection of the magical arrangement. He then himself fell bedridden for 9 months afterwards (perhaps harmed for his intervention). All in all, it does not matter whether we dismiss this as mere superstitious formula and the following affliction as psychosomatic production: either way, the Night does its work, proving that affective power has no concern for authenticity (only instigation).)

We are therefore already not far from understanding the complicated alignments and agitations that make up the referenced gesture of extispicy in the above verse: at its most basic level, extispicy refers to the ancient Mesopotamian practice of reading animal organs spattered upon a wall's surface. This inspection of entrails (often a sheep's liver) is a bygone approach to forensic study, akin to today's analysis of bloodstain patterns at a crime scene; yet it is a discipline of sacrificial desecration involved less with knowing than with watching, gleaning, and tracing the visual motifs of the specimen. It means that the night-gods are indeed proprietors of legible events (though written in mangled script), their clues residing in the manifest designs and streaks of the dismembered. It means that the lacerating rehearsal of the Magus brings its own test-drive (of the limits of power), and that the loaded concepts of divination, futurity, and truth are linked to a certain nocturnal awareness of the trickling, smearing, and rivulets of things.

Egyptian Night: Reckoning, Shackling, Breaking

When the fiends of Set come and change themselves into beasts, the great sovereign princes...slay them in the presence of their gods therein, and their blood floweth among them as they are smitten down.
The Egyptian Book of the Dead [75]

The principal focus of this section belongs to *The Egyptian Book of the Dead* and its cautious plotting of different night-occasions, including the: Night of Battle; Night of Reckoning Destruction; Night of Carrying Out Sentences; Night of Him Who Concealeth Himself; Night of Shackling Fiends; Night of Keeping Watch; Night of Festival (Haker); Night of the Things of the Night, and; Night of Breaking and Turning Up of the Earth. In order to extract whatever counter-concepts, then, we will study less the Egyptian gods' backstories than their telling epithets which together complete the stages of fatal procession through the underworld.

The Egyptian deities alleged to carry a specific phenomenological partnership with Night each boast their own occult conventions (modes of pandering, stimulation, or rune). Furthermore, their individual landscapes shift across meadows, gutters, and wombs with astounding narrative-theoretical flexibility, not to mention their physical orientations (some slither, hunch, fly, or remain seated). Preceding all other examples, however, is the internally two-sided force known as Kuk and Kauket: they are the first gods of obscurity, disorder, darkness, and void, masculine and feminine counterparts with frog and serpent heads respectively, living in an oceanic abyss and holding membership in the Ogdoad of Hermopolis (the original eight paired creator-gods of water, invisibility, infinity, and night) sired by Shu (name meaning "emptiness"). While Kuk controls the hours before dawn, Kauket rules the hours of twilight, their amphibian-reptilian faces perhaps a residual trace from even earlier cosmogonies related to Nile River crocodile gods. But what interests us most in terms of conceptual breakthroughs are the following five details which upend most traditional metaphysics: (1) that they supposedly died willingly after fulfilling their creational roles, receding back into primeval darkness upon serving their one purpose (the god who voluntarily perishes); (2) that the frog-man and snake-woman couple do not represent dualistic entities, as commonly interpreted, but rather a form of pendulous, collaborative interaction (the god who splits in order to extend fluidly); (3) that these pre-world figures do not reside on Olympian heights but rather in the subterranean below (the god who lives underneath); (4) that their epithets of "Bringer-in-of-Light" and "Bringer-in-of-Dark" supplant all notions of unifying, eternal time with windows of ever-splintering, transitional time (the god who wills temporal slits and passages); (5) that these night-deities still steer the sun-barge safely into netherworlds each evening, such that they continue exerting profound influence even in their deathliness (the god who moves worldly being from the grave's deficit).[76]

The next generation of Egyptian gods provides us with three further nocturnal identities: Nut, Khonsu, and Nephthys. To provide a brief synopsis, Nut is initially praised as goddess of the night sky, often depicted as a star-covered nude woman or cow arching over the earth, her hands and feet forming the cardinal points of north, south, east, and west. Her symbol is the ladder, and her name is inscribed on the sarcophagus of Queen Nefertari in the following invocation: "Descend, mother Nut, stretch out over my body and place me among the eternal stars within you, so that I may never die."[77] Noticeably, the goddess's multiple epithets — "Coverer of the Sky," "She Who Protects," "Mistress of All," "She Who Bore the Gods," and "She Who Holds a Thousand Souls" — also reinforce an integral aspect of the preceding supplication: namely, that her methodology of governance involves the literal engulfing of her followers. By extension, Night does rule from transcendent distances but rather envelops and swallows whole the existent into its gut or uterus (note the pharaonic queen's desire to be "within" her lord). To perceive universal space itself as divine innards: And what drastic conceptual shifts occur when re-orienting metaphysics away from a patriarchal gaze and into a maternal stomach, as all faith becomes a practice of immortal digestion?

The deity Khonsu also merits brief inclusion for certain reasons: as the moon-god, he supervises the nightly expedition of the lunar orb across the cosmos, but also surprisingly is deceived into gambling away portions of his moonlight to the god of magic/writing (Thoth) in a dice game. He is often depicted as mummified, wearing a fortune-bringing necklace, crook and scepter in hand, with only a curled, royal sidelock of hair showing on his facial profile; his sacred creature is the baboon; he is primarily invoked for healing or defense against wild animals; his epithets are the Traveler, Embracer, Pathfinder, Defender, and He Who Lives on Hearts (related to his devouring of pharaoh's enemies). Perhaps most interestingly, though, is that he is sometimes referred to as Khonsu the Child while also appealed to as a god of childbirth: thus the figure of the divine child (not the adult) rules over conception and delivery. A strange concoction of ideas thereby follows this night-wandering god: according to whatever titles and storylines, he is at once bloodthirsty (eating placenta and organs of royal opponents), merciful (protecting night-travelers and women in labor), and innocent (foolishly indifferent to his duties when distracted by schemes of luck and celestial betting). Cruelty, compassion, playful negligence; a shape-shifting god who resembles his own waning moon, and who would avenge, forgive, or hazard his cosmic share depending on his changing whims.

In close relation to the aforementioned figures is the goddess Nephthys, about whom less is known save her connective lineages (daughter of Nut, from whom she derives nocturnal powers), her sorority (sister of Isis, with whom she enacts all funerary rites), her marriage (wife of the untrusted Set, god of disarray, foreignness, and the desert), and her progeny (mother of the jackal-headed Anubis, guardian of cemeteries). She is a deity tied explicitly to the Night of the soul's traversal, portrayed symbolically as kite or falcon wings, a protector of sepulchral towers whose hieroglyphic allusions place her always in the direct presence of death, morbidity, and water. As the following Pyramid Text invites: "Ascend and descend; descend with Nephthys, sink into darkness with the Night-bark."[78] Beyond this, she is ascribed the roles of both priestess and divine nursemaid, feared for having breath of fire yet celebrated for collecting the amputated body parts of Osiris, and ultimately known to endow pharaohs with the vision for "that which is hidden by moonlight."[79] Nevertheless, it is her two most prominent epithets that allow us to comb through novel conceptual sites — "Lady of the Temple Enclosure" and "Queen of the Embalmer's Shop" — for these uneven banners in simultaneity allow us to see the altar and the autopsy table as one, the Magus and the corpse-washer, the temple and the morgue. Thus we should ask about the balancing-act between life and ending: What if all moments are actually just sinuously pouring death, both metaphysics and mortal existence coursing toward a cadaver's preparation for recoil, and all language (sacred or profane) the chorus of wailing women? All philosophy thereafter becomes an uncontroversial matter of the already-gone.

(Note: To highlight the Egyptian night-pantheon and its sky zodiac, one might also consider the brilliant astronomical contours of the Hathor Temple at Dendera—its pillars, halls, obelisks, columns, and ceilings adorned with turquoise representations of 12 female divinities in wave-like gowns (each one assigned to a particular hour of the night). Thus temporality was already perceived as a circuitous business of allotments, shares, and partial allocations.)[80]

Although less a god-force than a malevolent creature for the ages, we might simply note Apep as a giant sea-snake said to lurk again in the primordial gloom and the Tenth Region of Night, an enemy of the light-god (Ra), though formed from his nemesis's umbilical cord, who dwells below horizons and whose underground motions cause earthquakes, and whose epithets include "Serpent from the Nile," "Evil Lizard," and "World Encircler." Still, most productive for our conceptual experiment with Night is the presence of an instruction manual of the ancient Egyptian priests for defeating Apep: titled *The Books of Overthrowing Apep* (or by its Greek translation, the *Book of Apophis*), it details the intricate stages of combat, including "Spitting Upon Apep, Defiling Apep with the Left Foot, Taking a Lance to Smite Apep, Fettering Apep, Taking a Knife to Smite Apep, and Putting Fire Upon Apep."[81] The tactical arrangements span from base-material outputs (spit) to elemental properties (fire) to man-made weaponries (lance, knife) to fetishistic physiologies (the left foot) to sympathetic magic (tearing apart of effigies), each allowing the human participant to assist in the cosmic maiming of a being steeped in murkiness and muddy outer realms.

At long last, *The Egyptian Book of the Dead* allows us to contrive an unparalleled philosophy of Night, dusk, and shadow, notably providing several points of departure along the same lines of creative epithets enlisted thus far. Each division of Night carries its own reverberation for the now and then, the here and there, of the vague moods at stake in all fatal experience.

Thus we begin reading of "the night of the battle...the inroad [of the children of the impotent revolt] into the eastern part of heaven, whereupon there arose a battle in heaven and in all the earth."[82] The Night of the Battle places us in unmistakable sectarian logic, for which revolutionary territoriality at once rapidly sweeps over both worldly and otherworldly space while carving it into factional slivers (note the concomitance of "all the earth" and "eastern part" in the same articulation).

This Night of Battle, however, is on the very same page qualified as "the night of reckoning destruction, it is the night of the burning of the damned, and of the overthrow of the wicked at the block, and of the slaughter of souls."[83] Thus we uncover a principle of righteous carnage, for which the most pure brokers somehow become capable of the most gruesome deeds: the more grotesque the method, the more hallowed the event. This model neither resembles the sadistic serial killings of an Inquisition nor the paranoiac waves of witch burnings, but rather hinges only on a desire for clear reactional materiality (whatever heightens bleeding, flailing, shrieking). Without the complications of anxious psychology that accompany subjective demonstrations of power, this Night of Battle exports a simpler curiosity toward the other's receptivity, backlash, and reciprocity (the feeling-out of pressure-points).

Moving onward, we encounter a corresponding reference to "the night of the things of the night, and on the night of the battle, and on the night of the shackling of the Sebau fiends...,"[84] which interjects thingness, fiendishness, and monstrosity into our midst. This teratological and semi-demonological turn finally links Night to evil (though through its vanquishing) while also further introducing the concept of chaining (and how does one bind the tenebrous?). But Sebau as fanged being constitutes more than just obstacle: rather, it is anathema to Osiris's quest for invincibility through nightly resurrection. It renders the indefinite definite; it makes Being subside once and for all; in doing so, it threatens metaphysics to the core by instituting absolutely terminality (no next step, no beyond, no return), a nihilistic force of closure and irreversibility that if victorious would render all godliness obsolete.

Beyond this confrontation with the many leviathans of nullity, we come upon "the night when Isis lays down to keep watch in order to make lamentation for her brother Osiris."[85] This Night of Keeping Watch and Lamentation marks a certain festival, known also as "the night of the god Haker" for which all revel in "the rising up of joy in Teni (This)."[86] The particular mythic content of the event is less important, though, than the sheer fact of the carnivalesque, the spectacle, and the hyper-performance that now accompanies our study of ancient Night. More precisely, we have stepped over the cliffs from orthodoxy to dramaturgy: the solemnized rites of fasting and feasting are set to play-act the death and rebirth of Osiris, thereby confirming the role of simulation or passion-play as central to the tasks of nocturnal vigilance (keeping watch) and universal mourning (lamentation). And the fact that such extreme anxiety (becoming-lookouts) and extreme sorrow (becoming-elegists) somehow culminate in "joy" points to an improbable conceptual curvature: namely, that at the farthermost banks of this cosmic tale-telling, all existential tragedies of the soul convert themselves into ecstatic propulsions of the body (operational logic of entrancement).

Let us advance a new theory of fanatical sovereignty at work in pagan thought, one that would paradoxically entail both the ultimate keeping of the law and the ultimate violation of the law by its source (wrath of the ultimatum). Thus it is in the "presence of the sovereign princes" that we find interspersed both "the night of the carrying out of the sentence upon those who are to die"[87] and also "the night of the breaking and

turning up of the earth in their blood."[88] Hence, one-half of the
nocturnal equation is to uphold and seal the iron-clad edict of
the gods, particularly with respect to condemning the ill-fated
to their final demise, while the other half suggests a divine rage
that would precisely override itself to raze the very domain
of creation. Both are forms of zealotry—the first of keeping-
promise and the second of unruliness—that together bring us
to the following conceptual edge: that there are certain nights
when the most brutal enforcement of the gods' regulations then
wrenches sideways into rancor, spite, and the retaliatory desire
to shatter presiding structures. This is not the standard axiom
whereby the sovereign figure constitutes that which resides
above obedience to its own mandate (in a kind of hypocritical
free-zone), but rather an experiential level of sovereignty at
which the gods begin to express unbelievable hatred for their
own laws. As such, we find no contradiction between the Night
of Carrying Out Sentences and the Night of the Breaking and
Turning Up of the Earth: rather, they blend into one another
as sequential phases of nocturnal will, the fine line between
obsessive form and apocalyptic formlessness, as the saturation
of the first dimension (judgment) leads to the insatiability of the
second dimension (apoplexy).

The final stratum in this great tome of the dead concerns "the
night of him who concealeth himself in divers forms"[89], which
shows how the crafty minds of ancient civilizations already
resolved the dilemma of modern metaphysics and ideology:
namely, it reconciles the toxic dialectics of presence and
absence behind every theo-political order, and continuing into
our current epoch, by envisioning gods who instead disguise
themselves within the world as assortments (of miscellaneous
parts). Rather than occupy a discourse of empyreal hiddenness
and abstraction, which always overcompensates for its weak
intangibility through ultra-tangible displays of punishment
(beheading, burning, crucifixion), these gods walk among us

in immanent ambush, each one hiding in night's open view as a pack, legion, or wardrobe of many faces, masks, tongues, robes, tastes, proportions, and gestures. They do not recede into convenient bubbles of the unseen/unspoken, but rather adopt infinite visages, apparels, pseudonyms, and dialects in order to avoid the monochrome trappings of daily identity.

Persian Night: False World (The Trap)

The perverted, devilish, unrighteous rite of the "mystery of the sorcerers" consists in praising Ahriman, the destroyer.
The Dēnkard (Mazdaen Zoroastrian Text)[90]

The Zoroastrian supernatural being Angra Mainyu (later known as Ahriman in Middle Persian) is said to mislead minds into darkness, the "daeva of daevas" (etymological root of deviant/ devil) who persecutes worlds at nightfall. He is a figure of the omnimalevolent side: the first "destructive spirit," one of the antithetical twins of the primeval choice, opponent of the light and fire-god, creator of death, evil by personal wish, teaching humans only "worst thought" and fomenting crises of perception, dwelling in non-being, a shape-stealer whose name is written upside-down in distaste, sensorially associated with stench and noise, with depraved tendencies for self-cutting and the cooking of his own paranormal tissue. According to rarer accounts like the above passage, there were also cult rituals in Ahriman's (dis)honor whereby those involved would crush "a mortar herb called omomi, invok[ing] Hades and darkness; then having mingled it with the blood of a slaughtered wolf, they bear it forth into a sunless place and cast it away."[91] Suave admixtures of the shamans of the dark.

Nevertheless, the greatest conceptual payoff to be derived from all Ahrimanic allegories perhaps rests in the notion of earthly creation as mere ruse, net, and temporary prison for the night-god devised by his light-filled adversary Ahura Mazda. Thus worldly existence as we know it (and by extension all human life) is just decorative window-dressing to lure the false god away from its true cosmological battlefield and into a futile contest of wills…the entertainment of a useless physical plane. Thus a Zoroastrian theologian writes: "By his very struggles in the trap and snare, the beast's power is brought to nothing."[92] This single narrative maneuver hurls us into a theoretical whirlpool of illest consequence, for it spells the end of all human-interested metaphysics; it also displaces the earth's once-central orientation to the heavens; rather, we become pawns in a celestial side-game, our corporeal being a feint and hook, our souls' rise and fall a hunter's diversion to bait his eternal prey. Mortal transactions (civilizational, philosophical, religious, and moral trials) are thereby posed as but decoys, pitfalls, webs, fireworks displays, and baubles to attract a villain's gaze away from its rightful target.

Arabian Night: Violent Asceticism (The Raid)

These two altars have been made [i.e. erected] by 'Ubaidu son of 'Animu son of Saadallat, a Nabataean of the Rawaha (tribe), who was a horseman at Hirta and in the camp of 'Ana, to Shai' al-qaum, the good and bountiful god, who does not drink wine.
Altar Inscription (AD 132), Palmyra[93]

If we walk the vistas of Arabian sand dunes, at last we come upon a deity that enables us to think through the abiding relation between nocturnality and violence: al-Qaum, Nabataean god of war and night, guardian of caravans, his stern face carved into rock stelae and mountain-wall blocks, pre-Islamic "protector of the clan" and caretaker of the desert sleepers. But the above inscription, left upon a cavalryman's altar at Palmyra in the year

AD 132, interjects another angle into a tradition of night-gods otherwise bound to carnivorous, cannibalistic, and menacing forces: that of divine asceticism. The god of no drink, who self-restrains and disciplines, trims himself down in a kind of willed shyness, imbibes nothing, indulges nothing, in order to attain the correct level of combative readiness. Accordingly, al-Qaum observes the same code as those traders, nomads, and soldiers who worship him across long, deprived distances; they adhere to a regimen of the proponent or reserve fighter, and approximate the hard temporalities of the "in store," "on command," "lying in wait," and "at a breath's notice." Consequently, it is not really about the abstinence from desire, but rather about the isometric training/exercise of all impulses into a single desire for nocturnal fierceness: asceticism of the warrior, asceticism of the night-watchman, brought together in a perfect iteration of assault (the night-raid). (Note: Al-Qaum is also oppositionally linked to Shalim, Canaanite god of dusk (known for ravenous appetite and peace-making), while analogously linked to Aglibol ("Calf of the Lord"), early Arabian god of the moon shown often in military attire and with sickle in hand.)[94]

(Side-Story: Let us transcribe here another tale recounted by my wife's mother, this time about her father's sworn witnessing of the miraculous event of a *jinn*'s night-wedding (the jinn being a supernatural race in Arabian mythology known for causing mischief or possession, their name literally meaning "to conceal" and which later forms the anglicized "genie"). According to the story, one evening he went to water his family's agricultural lands and orchards when he heard the sound of loud drums and music in a nearby abandoned castle. He entered the castle to discover no people present nor any sign of an actual gathering except for the sonic bursts coming from behind a massive wooden door. He knocked on the door and was greeted by a local townsperson who he recognized as a remote acquaintance; the man smiled and beckoned him forward, telling him that he would soon share what was happening inside. Upon entering, they beheld a marriage feast of many guests, colored lanterns strung across rafters, and all kinds of delicacies spread throughout the inner room. He then noticed the bride and groom sitting on an elevated pedestal— both appearing with extraordinary, unearthly beauty—but was shocked to observe his own deceased wife's dress on the bride's body. He remarked astonished to the townsman from the door that it was the very same garb, but the latter assured him not to worry and that all would be restored to its proper place by morning. The townsman then warned, however, that the guest could partake of all the marvelous excesses of the celebration as long as he simply withheld from uttering the one phrase he said at every table before and after meals. He sat down on the banquet floor confused, not exactly inferring the referenced expression, picked up a bowl of food and from habit recited the opening Qur'anic prayer lines "In the name of Allah (God), the Most Compassionate, the Most Merciful." Upon speaking the blessed words, the entire wedding party instantly vanished and he was left in the dark castle alone again; he stood quickly and went running outside, shaking with fright from the scene of the lost festivity, realizing now that this dancing entourage had been for a ceremonial union of the jinn. The next day he found his wife's dress hanging in its usual closet corner and went in search of the townsperson who had played host the night before, only to hear from others that the same individual had left (no one knowing when) and could no longer be found.)

Cimmerian Night: Hypnotic Language (The Whisper)

And she made the outer limits, the Ocean River's bounds
where Cimmerian people have their homes—their realm and city
shrouded in mist and cloud. The eye of the Sun can never
flash his rays through the dark and bring them light,
not when he climbs the starry skies or when he wheels

back down from the heights to touch the earth once more—
an endless, deadly night overhangs those wretched men.
The Odyssey, Book XI[95]

The Cimmerians were an ambiguous, relatively short-lived civilization from the northern steppes of the Black Sea, most likely of Iranian origin and dispersed by the Scythians in the seventh century BC.[96] This notwithstanding, the exponential disinformation of legend is perhaps more conceptually helpful than the few scraps of historically-verified record at our disposal, for Homer's first vivid stab at a people entrenched in unending literary Night allows all sorts of associations to follow in kind: for instance, that the Cimmerians' intimacy with sunless limits placed them geographically at the suspected cave's mouth to the land of the dead, while also making them proficient at blind swordplay, scaling tall cliffs in pitch-darkness, and even conversing in the secret language of Night itself. And yet, the Cimmerians themselves are described as just killing, murmuring semblances (of what the dimness elicits), appearing as what humans are supposed to be but with no greater claim to ontological character: for this is what "wretched" pertains to here—being so dominated by external nature ("endless, deadly night") that one never develops a single shred of personal identity. Whereas the first Greek heroes were described as manic or sociopathic individualists—Achilles' rage, Odysseus' cunning—their same patron author Homer had no difficulty conceiving a people wholly bereft of psychology. That they learn to talk with Night is not indicative of a knowing subject, nor is it parcel of an "unconscious structured like a language," but rather of a nocturnal tongue that flicks itself beyond both consciousness and its repressed sub-layers (to become both hypnotized and hypnotic whisper). Perhaps the Cimmerian Night is therefore a communication by sound, sensation, and mood rather than by meaning, grammar, and comprehension; or even a language of subtle movements (temperature drops, intermittent gusts of air and wind, snapping of tree branches, shooting comets of sky).

Sabaean Night: Mind-Bending (The Riddle)

When the queen of Sheba heard about the fame of Solomon and his relationship to the LORD, SHE CAME TO TEST SOLOMON WITH HARD QUESTIONS.
The Bible, 1 Kings 10 [97]

The Sabaeans were flourishing spice-traders and star-worshipers in the Yemenite kingdom of Saba from approximately 1200-800 BC, a group whose fractal beliefs included building seven temples for each of the seven planets of the solar system, and each temple constructed with its own unique geometric design, color, ritual, and metallic substance. These planetary temples alone are enough to satisfy the basic criterion of nocturnality (for the galactic icons come out only at night), but our conclusive interplay of concepts comes at the hands of their empress, the infamous Queen of Sheba, mentioned vaguely throughout Jewish, Christian, and Islamic holy texts. There are of course many disagreeing interpretations of her visit to King Solomon given across centuries and sacred cultures—the particular gifts she offered, the aesthetics of the throne room at Solomon's palace, her varying promises, affirmations, and riches—but one detail remains steadfast throughout: the riddle. It is said that she arrived that first evening to test his mind, placing thought into distortion and misshapen knots while speaking into late hours.

So it is that Sheba becomes the embodied consul of intuition, filtered through Bronze Age and Iron Age eschatologies; she is the understudy of the careworn thinker (lost-in-thought), rendering consciousness increasingly difficult, non-durable, and anti-heuristic. Her riddles are finessed micro-events, allowing fringe sentiments to attack dogmatic maxims; her riddles tease rectified judgment into deliberative serpentines; her riddles are teleological attractors to the invidiousness of the mind's Night; her riddles encode the savage's love of impasse and failed speech (to choke the substrate). Here language never argues, only propositions; it drinks deep of the bifurcated and trifurcated remark. The Sabaeans thereby fasten Night back to the trick question-and-answer, these little games of mystification, amid the encounter between a monotheistic servant (King of Wisdom) and cosmic idolater (Queen of Riddles).

Concept Map (of the Apotheotic Night; dark concepts)

I.
BABYLONIAN NIGHT
Silence, Injustice, Divination

II.
EGYPTIAN NIGHT
Reckoning, Shackling, Breaking

III.
PERSIAN NIGHT
False World (The Trap)

IV.
ARABIAN NIGHT
Violent Asceticism (The Raid)

V.
CIMMERIAN NIGHT
Hypnotic Language (The Whisper)

VI.
SABAEAN NIGHT
Mind-Bending (The Riddle)

Ahmad Emad El-Din (Egypt). "Pharaonic Era" (2015).

Conclusion

Martyr's Night (dark thought)

* This conclusion contains the final premises of the manuscript—those of the dying-at-night, and the dead-of-night—by seizing upon the historical episode of an obscure, early twentieth-century guerilla leader who fled into the mountains and froze to death beneath the night sky. This image alone is enough to move toward a last philosophy of night, and a philosophy of the last night.

* * *

Night finds its smallest, delicate reflection in the eyes of a martyred man.

To locate his photograph one Night, by will or by chance, is to sink thought into a certain agony.

For the Night is tied to tragic patterns.

The martyr's eyes are kind, enough to know this story will go badly.

But his night-perishing allows us to embark upon a kind of conceptual fairytale.

For the Night is tied to the storyteller's sorrow (that all ends).

We first picture him in the forests at Night—hiding, starving, bone-cold, sleeping on wet earth.

He is devoted to acts of rebellion; he fights a cruel king, and uses shadow to conceal his movements.

For the Night is tied to stealth.

These long Nights beneath the trees are ripe for specific kinds of thought.

Thoughts of obvious separation (from family, lovers), thoughts of potential victory and loss (fatalistic struggle); but then also increasingly strange thoughts, of the futility of human experience amid insects and animals creeping in his midst. His hands, knuckles, fingernails seem transfigured.

This contemplative solitude in Night is an almost-lysergic sensation.

For the Night is tied to wondering.

We find him years later, storming cities at Night—he is running, his breath heavy like the gun slung across his right shoulder.

He is taller than most, and crouches to avoid detection, until rising to strike down the royal guards and soldiers. He kills on such rare night-occasions, though the photograph captures eyes that do not savor violence. No pleasure-principle of revolutionary vengeance, and one dreams that he holds a gentle touch even in acts of requisite murder.

For the Night is tied to uprising.

By Night, his bands descend from their elevated clearances to steal into the homes of feudal lords.

He is capable of anger. He takes the abusers hostage and ransoms their safe return for large sums that are then awarded to the poor, the starving, and the oppressed.

Still, his political orientations do not interest us. We are here only to seek his relation to the dimness that encircles his subversive actions, and that seemingly finds its way into a single image taken while others are fast asleep.

We are here for the secret of his radical softness.

For the Night is tied to both possession and dispossession.

Nearly a decade of nights filled with fragile triumph—he has sealed his rural outworld from outside forces; he has barricaded

105

his people within this green sanctuary for as long as his faction can resist.

His name becomes associated with legend, spoken by night fires in the surrounding lands.

He is already more a phantom image than a man, which spells the first drop of terminality in store.

Not much time left now.

For the Night is tied to countdown.

In this black-and-white photograph from around 1920, we stare directly into the dark pupils of someone for whom death is imminently near: the soon-to-die, the dying-young, the dying-too-early. Or is it, as another wondrous casualty once said, a matter of dying at the right time?

This martyr will meet an awful crossing one Night soon; it is almost as if there could be no other way; his face follows the evanescing moon in the Northern provinces.

For the Night is tied to disappearance.

The Night eventually reminds him of eventuality itself.

The martyr cannot prolong the inevitable burning-out of his tale, for Night has its own type of greed: it is a collector, it hoards the most precious, making a garland of the once-brave.

He was the leader of the Jungle Movement; now the jungle will confiscate him (never aging past his 41st birthday).

For the Night is tied to abdication.

The Night of final siege happens that same winter, compelling him to flee into nearby hills.

The martyr stays, endures; he has been here before and has mastered waiting.

His hair and beard have grown long and untamed; his lungs seize amid low temperatures.

He lays down for a while at one midnight's threshold, his

white exhalations crystallizing in the pitch-black air. He is calm as his body goes numb; the snow forms his burial shroud.

He dies of frostbite in the mountains in 1921.

For the Night is tied to dismay.

The Night of collection occurs amid distasteful methods, as an aristocratic governor takes the frozen body and gifts its amputated head to the new military-king.

His half-closed eyes are still beautiful, even in grotesque contexts.

There are two distinct images on record of this martyr's severed head, sent to a petty ruler to adorn his table and then placed atop a drawbridge in the capital city.

As if all reality were based on such symbolic displays of power; nothing save ominous reminders.

When we envision his detached crown, we hang our own heads in mimetic shame.

For the Night is tied to obscenity.

Against the poor sun of ideological regimes, we have the Night of the martyr's gaze to inspire.

But inspiration is something akin to madness, a mixture of horoscope and puppetry (tactics of the willed unknown). Psychoanalysis places far too great a causal importance on traumatic experience, since it has always suffered from the early prejudice of thinking madness only at its psychopathic extremes. But what Night demonstrates is that a certain sensitivity to lower-grade intimations can result in the gaining of more subtle lunatic powers: slight paranoiac ability, slight manic ability, slight delusional ability, slight schizophrenic ability, slight obsessive ability, slight melancholic ability. These are enchanted and revitalizing properties, for which Night provides the correct minimalist triggers and low-dose insinuations to bring the mind elsewhere.

Let this prospect conclude our many explorations of the later hours, then; let it all come to rest in the forgotten sadness and obscure eyes of a lone being destined to die at Night, both by its hands and for its sake. To become the dead-of-night.

Mirza Kuchak Khan (Jangali). Gilan Province, Iran. 1880-1921.

Appendix

Night-Supplements

I.

"It is night: alas that I must be light! And thirst for the nocturnal! And loneliness!"
Friedrich Nietzsche, "Night Song" in *The Portable Nietzsche* (New York: Penguin, 1977).

II.

"October 18, 1917. Dread of night. Dread of not-night."
Franz Kafka, *The Blue Octavo Notebooks* (New York: Exact Change: 2004), 13.

III.

"If I had known nothing of ecstasy before the object, I would not have attained ecstasy in the night. But *initiated* as I was in the object—and my initiation had represented the furthest penetration of the possible—I could only, in the night, find a deeper ecstasy."
Georges Bataille, *Inner Experience* (Albany: SUNY Press, 1988), 125.

IV.

"See black! Not that all your suns have fallen—they have since reappeared, only slightly dimmer—but Black is the 'color' that falls eternally from the Universe onto your Earth."
Francois Laruelle, *On the Black Universe: In the Human Foundations of Color* in *Hyun Soo Choi: Seven Large-Scale Paintings* (New York: Thread Waxing Space, 1991): 2-4, 7.

V.

"Night is falling. Ever since the 'united three'—Herakles, Dionysos, Christ—have left the world, the evening of the world's age has been declining toward its night. The world's night is spreading its darkness. The era is defined by the god's failure to arrive, by the 'default of God.'"
Martin Heidegger, "What Are Poets For?" in *Poetry, Language, Thought* (New York: Harper Perennial: 2001), 89.

VI.

"In the nocturnal life, there are depths where we bury ourselves, where we have the will to live no longer...We become beings with no history upon entering into the realm of the Night which has no history...Dreams without a history, dreams which could light up only in a perspective of annihilation are in the Nothing or in the Water. There the subject loses his being; they are dreams without a subject. Where is the philosopher who will give us a metaphysics of the night?"
Gaston Bachelard, *The Poetics of Reverie* (Boston: Beacon Press, 1971), 146-147.

VII.

"But when everything has disappeared in the night, 'everything has disappeared' appears. Night is this apparition: 'everything has disappeared.' This is the *other* night. It is what we sense when dreams replace sleep, when the dead pass into the deep of the night, when night's deep appears in those who have disappeared."
Maurice Blanchot, *The Space of Literature* (Lincoln: University of Nebraska Press, 1989), 163.

VIII.

"**Afraid of the Dark**. Nearly everyone can relate, I suspect, to the feeling of being 'afraid of the dark.' Sometimes we may be scared

of some unnamable thing *in* the dark, while at other times we may simply be scared *of* the dark itself…We do not know what it is that dwells in the darkness, only that our not-knowing is a source of fear. In short, our fear of the dark seems as ambiguous as darkness itself."
Eugene Thacker, *Starry Speculative Corpse* (Zero Books, 2015), 17.

IX.
"We shall see, in fact, that the ideal of the infinite is only an infinite which is tamed, harnessed and made palatable, and that radical limitlessness is made manifest not in sweet dreams, but in the void of a bottomless well and the nightmare of destruction…"
Francois Flahault, *Malice* (New York: Verso, 2003), 7.

X.
"As a result of the absorption of the 'dead star' into the 'lute,' the 'Black Sun' of 'Melancholia' emerges. Beyond its alchemical scope, the 'Black Sun' metaphor fully sums up the blinding force of the despondent mood—an excruciating, lucid affect asserts the inevitability of death, which is the death of the loved one and of the self that identifies with the former…"
Julia Kristeva, *Black Sun: Depression and Melancholia* (New York: Columbia University Press, 1992), 151.

XI.
"Keeping for the night your envy and your hate. But I want to interpret your midnight dreams, and unmask that phenomenon: your night. And make you admit that I dwell in it as your most fearsome adversary."
Luce Irigaray, *Marine Lover of Friedrich Nietzsche* (New York: Columbia University, 1991), 25.

XII.
"Oh and night: there is night, when a wind full of infinite space

gnaws at our faces. Whom would it not remain for—that longed-after, mildly disillusioning presence, which the solitary heart so painfully meets."

Rainer Maria Rilke, "Duino Elegies" in *The Selected Poetry of Rainer Maria Rilke* (New York: Vintage, 1989), 151.

XIII.

"You must stay up all night at least four times a year. There aren't enough crazy people around me to go further than that. A single sleepless night isn't worth much when you're on your own. It needs to be shared. Only then does the city open up to you without thoughts of death. Gargoyles carry out their work as exorcists. Muezzins get drunk on street corners. There is always a couple who get married at dawn by drawing lots. The Partisans' Chant becomes a drinking song. Satan starts to wax lyrical and hands out unbaited, red apples to the worshippers. Feet trample on a treasure-hoard of stars. The taste of sex rises in the mouth like lemon on oysters. Only vagabonds can be poets."

Abdellatif Laabi, "Burn the Midnight Oil" trans. Andre Naffis-Sahely (Poetry Translation Centre).

XIV.

When it comes, it brings with it a smell, a fragrance even. You learn to recognize it as a kid growing up in these narrow streets. You develop a knack for detecting it, tasting it in the air. You can almost see it. Like a witch's familiar, it lurks in the shadows, follows you at a distance wherever you go...Tonight, another one is starting.

Atef Abu Saif, *The Drone Eats With Me: A Gaza Diary* (Boston: Beacon Press, 2016), 1-2.

XV.

"The man scowls. His weariness makes him seem vulnerable to

me. I climb the three steps and then turn towards him.

Why didn't you have the courage to kill them? A normal man would have made short work of them."

His response surprises me: "But I kill them every night. I'm actually starting to get tired of it."
Ahmed Bouanani, *The Hospital* (New York: New Directions, 2018), 137.

XVI.
"Evening: The moon dancing, tumbling off the precipice of the universe. Did Lucifer know that she couldn't be touched? Even when she was decadent, mellowed, indecisive? Even when she fell into the lap of Eden, her white globular head tossing in the wind of stars, her face pressing into the bosom of yesterday's dream?"
Vi Khi Nao, *A Brief Alphabet of Torture* (Tuscaloosa: University of Alabama Press, 2017), 33.

XVII.
"After weeks of bombing we woke up one morning to find the sky pitch black. The smoke from the torched oil wells in Kuwait had obliterated the sky. Black rain fell afterward, colouring everything with soot as if forecasting what would befall us later...

Even the statues are too terrified to sleep at night lest they wake up as ruins."
Sinan Antoon, *The Corpse Washer* (New Haven: Yale University Press, 2014), 61/103.

XVIII.
"She wanted to challenge her patron saint on the promises he had given her, but she waited for the night to fall because during the day the picture was just a picture, inanimate and completely still, but at night a portal opened between her world and the other world."

Ahmed Saadawi, *Frankenstein in Baghdad* (New York: Penguin, 2018), 16.

XIX.

"Night deepens, and this is the question: Who's dreaming whom? A fault-line separates us from our share...

Last night, a stormy night, Hegel visited my sleep, and I heard him say, with a rhythmic voice, that 'man is this night, this empty nothingness: a wealth of infinite representations, images, none of which meant to be present to his spirit, or to be absent. It's night that exists here, (he continued), the intimacy of nature, the Self in all its purity'. He insisted in saying that 'night forms just a circle around man's imaginary representations: here a bloody head surging forth, there a white face, always disappearing brutally'. That's the night that we see (he told me) when we look a man in the eyes: we sink then in a night of terror, the night of the world is then facing us."
Etel Adnan, *Night* (New York: Nightboat, 2016), 28-30.

XX.

"The final darkness of the night envelops the city like a thin skin. Garbage trucks begin to appear on the streets. As they collect their loads and move on, people who have spent the night in various parts of the city begin to take their place, walking toward subway stations, intent upon catching those first trains that will take them out to the suburbs, like schools of fish swimming upstream. People who have finally finished the work they must do all night, young people who are tired from playing all night: whatever the difference in their situations, both types are equally reticent. Even the young couple who stop at a drink vending machine, tightly pressed against each other, have no more words for each other."
Haruki Murakami, *After Dark* (New York: Vintage, 2008), 222.

XXI.
"Ungrained night. Night of murder.
I shall not extend the deadline.
To kill God in his original light, the stars."
Edmond Jabes, *The Book of Questions* (Middletown: Wesleyan University Press, 1991), 61.

XXII.
"A phosphorescent jewel gives off its glow and color in the dark and loses its beauty in the light of day. Were it not for shadows, there would be no beauty."
Jun'ichirō Tanizaki, *In Praise of Shadows* (Sedgwick: Leet's Island Books, 1977), 46.

XXIII.
"And if I fall before night along the highway
Face against the ground and both arms outstretched
At the bottom of any silent influx of strength inside me
I will redress for the night of bewilderment
Roger Gilbert-Lecomte, *Black Mirror* (Barrytown: Station Hill Press, 2010), 95.

XXIV.
"To swallow the night in its very silence (which is not to say every silence) – a night that's immense, and immersed in the stealth of lost footsteps."
Alejandra Pizarnik, *Extracting the Stones of Madness* (New York: New Directions, 2016), 97.

Works Cited

Chapter 1

1   This chapter was first published under the title "The Night Traveler: Theories of Nocturnal Time, Space, Movement" in *Philosophy, Travel, and Place: Being In Transit*, eds. Ron Scapp and Brian Seitz (New York: Palgrave Macmillan, 2019)

2   Bernard Khoury (architect). B018. Beirut, Lebanon (1998). http://www.bernardkhoury.com/project.php?id=127

3   Larissa Sansour and Soren Lind (filmmaker). *In the Future, They Ate From the Finest Porcelain* (film, 2016). http://www.larissasansour.com/Future.html

4   Bernard Khoury (architect). B018. Beirut, Lebanon (1998). http://www.bernardkhoury.com/project.php?id=127

5   Bernard Khoury (architect). B018. Beirut, Lebanon (1998). http://www.bernardkhoury.com/project.php?id=127

6   The term "dead ringers" derives more accurately from an old practice of fraud in horse-racing, which prompts one to add another conceptual personage to the mix of nocturnal experience: the Horseman's Night.

7   Larissa Sansour and Soren Lind (filmmaker). *In the Future, They Ate From the Finest Porcelain* (film, 2016). http://www.larissasansour.com/Future.html

8   Larissa Sansour and Soren Lind (filmmaker). *In the Future, They Ate From the Finest Porcelain* (film, 2016). http://www.larissasansour.com/Future.html

9   Larissa Sansour and Soren Lind (filmmaker). *In the Future, They Ate From the Finest Porcelain* (film, 2016). http://www.larissasansour.com/Future.html

10   Larissa Sansour and Soren Lind (filmmaker). *In the Future, They Ate From the Finest Porcelain* (film, 2016). http://www.larissasansour.com/Future.html

11   Is the implication here that totalitarian systems remain

optimally uninoculated against the imperceptible travel of certain images, stories, and rumors (counter-scourge)... especially those traded by night?

Chapter 2

12 Yasunari Kawabata, *House of the Sleeping Beauties and Other Stories*, trans. E. Seidensticker (Tokyo: Kodansha International, 1969), 16.

13 This chapter was first published under the same title in the Journal of Comparative and Continental Philosophy (Taylor & Francis), Special Issue, *Soundproof Room*, ed. Jason Mohaghegh, 2019.

14 Ibid., 69

15 Ibid., 39

16 Ibid., 78

17 Ibid., 95

18 Note that this transactional logic holds only until the juncture where this contract is betrayed by an old man's actual death, for which the very next night a sleeping beauty must also actually die

19 Ibid., 20-23

20 Ibid., 43

21 Ibid., 58

22 Ibid., 76

23 Ibid., 96

24 Ibid., 97

25 Ibid., 80

26 Ibid., 13

27 Ibid., 98

28 Ibid., 85

Chapter 3

29 Christiane Gruber (trans.), *The Ilkhanid Book of Ascension: A Persian-Sunni Devotional Tale* (London: I.B. Tauris 2010), 34.

30 Note that the texts of night-journey and ascension also contain their own powerful meta-commentaries on Night itself, quoting from Qur'anic verses to establish a set of winding hermeneutic inroads. For instance, from the *Ilkhanid Book of Ascension* that dominates this chapter: "This ascent occurred at night because the command to serve is also at night. *'Stand (to prayer) by night.'* The order to call out the fairies (*pariyan*) also was at night. One night come to pray; another night to read [the Qur'an], and on the third come to tell your secrets. God gave to this lord four nights: the night of service, the night of invitation, the night of proof, and the night of witnessing."(82) Lord of the four nights: a complex philosophy awaits here, requiring further dissection and invention, ciphering and deciphering.

31 There are numerous scholarly works engaging the *isra'* (night-journey) and *mi'raj* (ascension), including: Frederick S. Colby (trans.), *The Subtleties of the Ascension* (Louisville: Fons Vitae, 2006); Frederick S. Colby, *Narrating Muhammad's Night Journey* (New York: SUNY Press, 2008); Christiane Gruber and Frederick Colby (eds.), *The Prophet's Ascension* (Bloomington: Indiana University Press, 2010); John Renard, *Friends of God* and *Tales of God's Friends* (Berkeley: University of California Press, 2008; 2009); Omid Safi, *Memories of Muhammad* (New York: Harper One, 2009); Michael Anthony Sells, *Early Islamic Mysticism* (Mahwah: Paulist Press, 1995).

32 Ibid., 37
33 Ibid., 38
34 Ibid., 39
35 Ibid., 40
36 Ibid., 42
37 Ibid., 44-45
38 Ibid., 44
39 Ibid., 45
40 Ibid., 46

41 Ibid., 48
42 Ibid., 50
43 Ibid., 52
44 Ibid., 52, 63
45 Ibid., 52
46 Ibid., 52
47 Ibid., 55, 56, 54, 55
48 Ibid., 55, 56, 55
49 Ibid., 53
50 Ibid., 53
51 Ibid., 58
52 Ibid., 81
53 Ibid., 60
54 Ibid., 62-63
55 Ibid., 63
56 Ibid., 65
57 Ibid., 62
58 Ibid., 68
59 Ibid., 65
60 Ibid., 64
61 Ibid., 59
62 Ibid., 70
63 Ibid., 70
64 Ibid., 71
65 Ibid., 67
66 Ibid., 67
67 "Bestami, Bayazid", entry in *Encyclopaedia Iranica*, Vol. IV, Fasc. 2, 183-186. http://www.iranicaonline.org/articles/best ami-bastami-bayazid-abu-yazid-tayfur-b

Chapter 4

68 Cited in Jeffrey L. Cooley, "An Old Babylonian Prayer to the Gods of Night," in *Reading Akkadian Prayers and Hymns: An Introduction* ed. A. Lenzi (Society of Biblical Literature,

2011), 82. It can also be found at the website of the SEAL Project of the Department of History, SOAS University of London.

69 Ibid., 82

70 Information regarding the Mesopotamian deities Shamash, Sin, Adad, Ishtar, Girra, and Erra is derived from a combination of the following works' contents: Stephanie Dalley (translator), *Myths from Mesopotamia: Creation, The Flood, Gilgamesh, and Others* (Oxford: Oxford World Classics, 2009); Jeremy Black and Anthony Green, *Gods, Demons and Symbols of Ancient Mesopotamia: An Illustrated Dictionary* (London: The British Museum Press, 1992); Glenn Stanfield Holland, *Gods in the Desert: Religions of the Ancient Near East* (New York: Rowman & Littlefield Publishers, 2009); *Encyclopaedia Britannica*; *Ancient History Encyclopedia*; and Ancient Mesopotamian Gods and Goddesses Project (http://oracc.museum.upenn.edu/amgg/)

71 https://www.britannica.com/topic/Ishtar-Mesopotamian-goddess

72 "Samael" in *A Dictionary of Angels, Including the Fallen Angels* by Gustav Davidson (New York: Simon & Schuster, 1999), 255

73 Cooley, Ibid., 82

74 Ibid., 82

75 Wallace Budge (translator), *The Egyptian Book of the Dead* (New York: Penguin Classics, 2008,) 121

76 Information regarding the ancient Egyptian deities Kuk, Kauket, Nut, Khonsu, Nephthys, and Apep is derived from a combination of the following works' contents: Geraldine Pinch, *Egyptian Mythology: A Guide to the Gods, Goddesses, and Traditions of Ancient Egypt* (Oxford: Oxford University Press, 2004); Richard H. Wilkinson, *The Complete Gods and Goddesses of Egypt* (London: Thames and Hudson, 2017); Gerald Massey, *Ancient Egypt: The Light of the World*

(Eastford, CT: Martino Fine Books, 2014); Charles R. Coulter and Patricia Turner, *Encyclopedia of Ancient Deities* (Jefferson, NC: McFarland and Company, 2000), and; various entries from *Encylopaedia Britannica*, *Wikipedia*, and *Ancient History Encyclopedia*

77 Nefertari's Tomb Inscription, Queens of Egypt Exhibition, Pointe-à-Callière Museum, Montreal, 2018

78 Pyramid Text Utterance 222 line 210 cited in R.O. Faulkner, *Ancient Egyptian Pyramid Texts* (Oxford: Oxford University Press, 1969)

79 A. Gutbub, J. Bergman, *Nephthys découverte dans un papyrus magique in Mélanges* (Montpelier, France: Publications de la recherche, université de Montpellier, 1984) cited in https://en.wikipedia.org/wiki/Nephthys

80 For superior images and descriptions of the Hathor Temple at Dendera, search the following link at: https://paulsmit.smugmug.com/Features/Africa/Egypt-Dendera-temple/

81 P. Kousoulis, *Magic and Religion as Performative Theological Unity: The Apotropaic Ritual of Overthrowing Apophis*, Ph.D. dissertation, University of Liverpool (Liverpool, 1999)

82 Wallace Budge (translator), *The Egyptian Book of the Dead*, 104

83 Ibid., 104

84 Ibid., 116

85 Ibid., 119

86 Ibid., 119

87 Ibid., 120

88 Ibid., 121

89 Ibid., 121-122

90 Dēnkard (p. 182.6) cited in J. Duchesne-Guillemin, "AHRIMAN," Encyclopædia Iranica, I/6-7, 670-673; an updated version is available online at http://www.iranicaonline.org/articles/ahriman (accessed on 28 March 2014)

91 Plutarch (*Isis and Osiris* 47) cited in J. Duchesne-Guillemin, "AHRIMAN," Encyclopædia Iranica

92 Zātspram 3.23 and Škand Gumānīg Vičār 4.63-79 [ed. J. de Menasce, Fribourg en Suisse, 1945]) cited in J. Duchesne-Guillemin, "AHRIMAN," Encyclopædia Iranica

93 Javier Teixidor, *The Pantheon of Palmyra* (Leiden: Brill Publishers, 1997), 86

94 Also see Jane Taylor, *Petra and the Lost Kingdom of the Nabateans* (Cambridge: Harvard University Press, 2002), 126

95 Homer. *The Odyssey* trans. Robert Fagles (New York: Penguin Classics, 1999), Book XI

96 Sergei R. Tokhtas'ev, "CIMMERIANS," Encyclopædia Iranica, V/6, 563-567, available online at http://www.iranicaonline.org/articles/cimmerians-nomads (accessed on 30 December 2012)

97 *The Holy Bible: New International Version* (Zondervan: Biblica, Inc. 2015), 1 Kings 10, NIV

CULTURE, SOCIETY & POLITICS

Contemporary culture has eliminated the concept and public figure of the intellectual. A cretinous anti-intellectualism presides, cheer-led by hacks in the pay of multinational corporations who reassure their bored readers that there is no need to rouse themselves from their stupor. Zer0 Books knows that another kind of discourse – intellectual without being academic, popular without being populist – is not only possible: it is already flourishing. Zer0 is convinced that in the unthinking, blandly consensual culture in which we live, critical and engaged theoretical reflection is more important than ever before. If you have enjoyed this book, why not tell other readers by posting a review on your preferred book site. Recent bestsellers from Zero Books are:

In the Dust of This Planet
Horror of Philosophy vol. 1
Eugene Thacker
In the first of a series of three books on the Horror of Philosophy, *In the Dust of This Planet* offers the genre of horror as a way of thinking about the unthinkable.
Paperback: 978-1-84694-676-9 ebook: 978-1-78099-010-1

Capitalist Realism
Is there No Alternative?
Mark Fisher
An analysis of the ways in which capitalism has presented itself as the only realistic political-economic system.
Paperback: 978-1-84694-317-1 ebook: 978-1-78099-734-6

Rebel Rebel
Chris O'Leary
David Bowie: every single song. Everything you want to know, everything you didn't know.
Paperback: 978-1-78099-244-0 ebook: 978-1-78099-713-1

Cartographies of the Absolute
Alberto Toscano, Jeff Kinkle
An aesthetics of the economy for the twenty-first century.
Paperback: 978-1-78099-275-4 ebook: 978-1-78279-973-3

Malign Velocities
Accelerationism and Capitalism
Benjamin Noys
Long listed for the Bread and Roses Prize 2015, *Malign Velocities* argues against the need for speed, tracking acceleration as the symptom of the ongoing crises of capitalism.
Paperback: 978-1-78279-300-7 ebook: 978-1-78279-299-4

Meat Market
Female Flesh under Capitalism
Laurie Penny
A feminist dissection of women's bodies as the fleshy fulcrum of capitalist cannibalism, whereby women are both consumers and consumed.
Paperback: 978-1-84694-521-2 ebook: 978-1-84694-782-7

Poor but Sexy
Culture Clashes in Europe East and West
Agata Pyzik
How the East stayed East and the West stayed West.
Paperback: 978-1-78099-394-2 ebook: 978-1-78099-395-9

Romeo and Juliet in Palestine
Teaching Under Occupation
Tom Sperlinger
Life in the West Bank, the nature of pedagogy and the role of a
university under occupation.
Paperback: 978-1-78279-637-4 ebook: 978-1-78279-636-7

Sweetening the Pill
or How We Got Hooked on Hormonal Birth Control
Holly Grigg-Spall
Has contraception liberated or oppressed women? *Sweetening
the Pill* breaks the silence on the dark side of hormonal
contraception.
Paperback: 978-1-78099-607-3 ebook: 978-1-78099-608-0

Why Are We The Good Guys?
Reclaiming your Mind from the Delusions of Propaganda
David Cromwell
A provocative challenge to the standard ideology that Western
power is a benevolent force in the world.
Paperback: 978-1-78099-365-2 ebook: 978-1-78099-366-9

Readers of ebooks can buy or view any of these bestsellers by
clicking on the live link in the title. Most titles are published
in paperback and as an ebook. Paperbacks are available in
traditional bookshops. Both print and ebook formats are available
online.
Find more titles and sign up to our readers' newsletter
at http://www.johnhuntpublishing.com/culture-and-politics
Follow us on Facebook
at https://www.facebook.com/ZeroBooks
and Twitter at https://twitter.com/Zer0Books